Ourselves in Southern Africa

An Anthology of
Southern African Writing

COMPILED BY ROBIN MALAN

Assistant Head and Head of English Department, Waterford Kamhlaba
United World College of Southern Africa, Swaziland

St. Martin's Press
New York

PR
9345
.O97
1989

Scholarly and Reference Division,
St. Martin's Press, Inc., 175 Fifth Avenue, New York, NY 10010

First published in the United States of America in 1989

Printed in Hong Kong

ISBN 0–312–03194–7

Library of Congress Cataloging-in-Publication Data
Ourselves in southern Africa : an anthology of southern African
    writing / compiled by Robin Malan.
        p.   cm.
Bibliography: p.
ISBN 0–312–03194–7
1. Southern Africa literature (English)   2. Africa, Southern–
–Literary collections.   I. Malan, Robin.
PR9345.097   1989
820'.9'968—dc19   89–6064
                                                              CIP

Photographic Acknowledgements
The author and publishers wish to acknowledge, with thanks, the following
photographic sources.
AFRAPIX, p 188 left (photograph Santu Mofokeng)
"The Argus" p 202 top right (photograph N.E.L.M.)
Bailey's African Archives p 200 left
Camera Press pp 187 left; 193 top left; 194 left; 200 right
Donker Publishers p 194 right (photograph N.E.L.M./Monica Fairall)
"The Evening Post", Post Elizabeth p 198 left
Fay Godwin p 190 left
Heinemann Education Books p 184 left
I.D.A.F. pp 187 right (photograph Dave Hartman); 197 right (photograph Jurgen
Schadenburg); 205 left; 205 right (photograph Jurgen Schadenburg)
N.E.L.M. pp 184 right (photograph Hepburn and Jeanes); 188 right; 190 right; 193
top right; 198 right; 202 bottom (photograph Robert Turney)
The publishers have made every effort to trace the copyright holders, but if they have
inadvertently overlooked any, they will be pleased to make the necessary
arrangements at the first opportunity.

Contents

Introduction

There is no doubt that a great deal has happened in the literature of Southern Africa in recent years. How could it be otherwise in a subcontinent as extraordinary as this one!

There used to be a time when South African English literature was dominated by the writings of white South Africans. It is not difficult to see how this came about.

Of course, there was writing in English by black writers, but this was not published by South African publishing houses, which seemed very much the preserve of whites. Black writers were dependent on being published in magazines, such as the epoch-making *Drum* magazine of the 1950s.

Then the trauma in 1960 of the shootings at Sharpeville and the subsequent State of Emergency and bannings caused large-scale exiling of many writers, who were then published abroad but banned in South Africa — the 1960s came to be known in South African writing as the Silent Decade. These writers included Peter Abrahams, Ezekiel (later Es'kia) Mphahlele, Alex la Guma, Dennis Brutus, Todd Matshikiza, Bloke Modisane, Can Themba.

Many of these writers are only now being 'discovered' by South African readers. New and much more enterprising South African publishing houses have succeeded in having the bans lifted and have now re-issued their work. It is a very odd experience for readers to be making a first acquaintance with work that was pertinent twenty years ago!

The emergence in print of black South African poets writing in English can be dated from 1971. Renoster Books published Mbuyiseni Oswald Mtshali's *Sounds of a Cowhide Drum* and Mongane Serote's *Yakhal' Inkomo*, and then Ad. Donker issued Robert Royston's anthology of black poets *To Whom it May Concern* and took over the two earlier works. The effect was profound: a great deal of 'protest' writing was published.

After 1976 this 'protest' poetry changed: its audience was now predominantly black, not white, and it became known as 'black consciousness' poetry. Much impetus was given by *Staffrider* magazine in the late 1970s and early 1980s. In the last decade and a half two major anthologies devoted to black South African poetry have been published (*Voices from Within* ed. Michael Chapman and Achmat Dangor, Ad. Donker, and *The*

Return of the Amasi Bird ed. Tim Couzens and Essop Patel, Ravan Press), and as many as forty-five individual volumes from thirteen publishers.

In the meantime great changes were happening all around South Africa: Mozambique, Angola, Lesotho, Botswana and Swaziland all achieved independence, and, after the Chimurenga War, Zimbabwe was born.

Great and stirring times! And through them all, the institutions of apartheid were being strengthened and the divisions between people were being entrenched and enforced.

In education, very little of the stirring times was reflected in the literature that students − of whatever colour − were having prescribed for them. If students studied the twentieth century at all, it was only in the 'veld and vlei' adventures of white short story writers.

Some of that has now changed. Some − mainly white − education authorities are acknowledging that there is a need for all sorts of Southern African students to be introduced to all sorts of Southern African writers. And black education in the formal sphere is in such a state of disarray that the community education and people's education now being formulated will surely see to it that the literature students read reflects the multi-faceted reality of Southern Africa today.

This collection hopes to find a place in all of these changed or changing arenas. It is designed to be appropriate to the Southern African situation in several different ways.

I think it is important that the literature Southern African students read now does more than a literary job: we actually need literature to enable our young people to get to know one another, to cut across and to break down the old 'separatenesses' that political, social and educational structures created.

I believe the breadth of experience offered by these pieces can achieve this.

The collection is deliberately a mixed anthology: there are poems, short stories, plays and a number of other forms represented here. So often prescriptions of Southern African literature have to be exclusive: either you are offered only short stories or only a number of poems. And so you miss the amazing diversity of what is being written in Southern Africa. So, poems are placed side by side with autobiographical pieces, newspaper articles, as well as short stories and extracts from longer pieces, novels, novellas or plays.

Geographically the writings and/or writers come from rural and urban South Africa, from Botswana, Swaziland, Zimbabwe.

And these are arranged around a number of themes, these serving only to gather related pieces together and not intending to force strait-jacketed reactions.

Selection decisions have to be made, of course; no anthology can include everything. For instance, I have not included work that is specific to the events of Soweto 1976, though I believe these events to make up a crucial moment in the creation of post-apartheid South Africa. The most important reason for this is that in 1986, the tenth anniversary of Soweto 1976, a number of anthologies and collections came on to the market. I think, for instance, of Siba Ndaba's *One Day in June*. So psychologically traumatic an event in the nation's history was Soweto 1976 (it's true: nothing has been the same since) that I am reluctant to select some five or six pieces from the considerable body of work that exists and pretend that 'this is Soweto 1976'.

A few words about the way the book is put together. There is a thin line of commentary inside each section, linking one piece to the next where this seems appropriate or necessary. Following each piece any notes thought necessary are given as brief footnotes. I have made use of Jean Branford's *A Dictionary of South African English* (Oxford University Press Cape Town 1980) and Dr Ridley Beeton and Helen Dorner: *A Dictionary of English Usage in Southern Africa* (OUP Cape Town 1975).

At the end of each section, some points for discussion or written consideration are offered. I hope students will find these useful and interesting, whether they are specifically required to give them their attention or not.

At the end of the collection, some biographical notes on the authors are added, together with lists of their works for further reading.

RM
Mbabane Swaziland
1987

Acknowledgements

The author and publishers wish to thank the following who have kindly given permission for the use of copyright material:—
Jonathan Cape Ltd on behalf of Nadine Gordimer for **The Bridegroom** from *Selected Stories* (1976)
Jeni Couzyn for her poem **In the house of the father** from *Christmas in Africa* (1975)
Ad Donker (Pty) Ltd for **Sweet-water** by Guy Butler from *Selected Poems* (1975); **One small boy longs for summer** by Mafika Gwala from *Jol'iikomo* (1977); **Dust** by Douglas Livingstone from *The anvil's undertone* (1978); **Amagoduka at Glencoe Station**, **An abandoned bundle** and **Boy on a swing** by Mbuyiseni Oswald Mtshali from *Sounds of a cowhide drum* (1973); **Next time** by Sheila Roberts from *Outside life's feast*; **Adriaanspoort** and **Hat's off in my house!** by Sipho Sepamla from *Hurry up to it!*; **Da same — da same** by Sipho Sepamla from *The blues is you in me* (1976); **I am the man** by Mongane Serote from *No Baby must weep* (1975); **The actual dialogue** by Mongane Serote from *Yakhal'inkomo* (1973/1972); **There will be a better time** by Mongane Serote from *Selected Poems* (ed. Mbulelo Mzamane) (1982); **Bye bye, overcoat** by Mutiswayo Shandu from *Quarry 80—82* (1982); **A Riot Policeman**, **In Detention** and **On learning Sotho** by Chris van Wyk from *It is time to go home* (1979).
Heinemann Educational Books Ltd for **Letters to Martha 4, 9, 10, 14** from *A simple lust* by Dennis Brutus (1973); an extract from **A walk in the night** from *A walk in the night and other stories* by Alex La Guma (1968); **The Dube Train** from *The will to die* (1982/83) by Can Themba; **The Wind and a Boy** from *The Collector of treasures* by Bessie Head (1977)
John Johnson Limited for **The prisoner who wore glasses** by Bessie Head from *On the edge of the world* (1974)
Mambo Press for **Important matters** and **Sitting on the balcony** by Charles Mungoshi and **Cattle in the rain** by Musaemura Zimunya from *Zimbabwean Poetry in English* (1981); **The Mount of Moriah** by Charles Mungoshi from *Some kinds of wounds* (1980)
A D Peters & Co Ltd for **Mr Drum goes to jail** by Henry Nxumalo from *Drum* by Anthony Sampson (1983) published by Hodder and Stoughton
David Philip Publisher (Pty) Ltd for **To Lucky with his guitar on a Grahamstown Street** by Chris Zithulele Mann from *New Shades* (1982, and **Words to the security police** by Alan Paton from *Knocking on the door* (1975)
Richard Rive for his story **Rain** and radio play **Make like slaves** from *Three South Africans Abroad* (1977)
Every effort has been made to trace all the copyright holders but if any have been inadvertently overlooked the publishers will be pleased to make the necessary arrangement at the first opportunity

Speaking of ourselves

Years of various kinds of 'separateness' have made it very difficult for many South Africans to speak to one another. Even if there was contact once, time and changing circumstances have made it a tricky thing for one man to talk to another:

Between Ourselves

Mike Kirkwood

> A pit yawns under our talk:
> each evening, a new subsidence,
> the words slipping helplessly further away.
>
> We look at each other across
> the gap no-one's responsible for.
> In the old days — fifty, a half dozen
> years ago — we knew how to blame
> each other, the krulkop calling
> the kafferboetie black, an old joke
> no-one now would care for. Instead each
> in his thought circles an identical
> and rueful vacancy, and we wait
> on midnight to cry or cackle in it.

Notes
krulkop — Afrikaans: curly-head, sometimes used in a derogatory way of black people, similar perhaps to 'gollywog'
kafferboetie — Afrikaans: literally it means 'kaffir-brother', used in a derogatory way of whites who are friendly to and with black people.
Kirkwood is punning on the expression 'the pot calling the kettle black'.

1

The Actual Dialogue

Mongane Serote

> Do not fear Baas.
> It's just that I appeared
> And our faces met
> In this black night that's like me.
> Do not fear —
> We will always meet
> When you do not expect me.
> I will appear
> In the night that's black like me.
> Do not fear —
> Blame your heart
> When you fear me —
> I will blame my mind
> When I fear you
> In the night that's black like me.
> Do not fear Baas,
> My heart is vast as the sea
> And your mind as the earth.
> It's awright Baas,
> Do not fear.

Note

baas — Afrikaans: 'Master'. It is not a word that finds general acceptance nowa-days. It is a word that works in only one direction — I have never heard of a white South African who calls a black man 'Baas'.

Yet, in the next three poems we see that people of different colours can and do respect one another and one another's beliefs:

Grave of Unknown Whiteman

Modikwe Dikobe

Rest in peace, old man
A heap of rocks on your grave
Is a token of respect
Bestowed on you.

You chose this part of the country
For a home
On a slope of those rocks
Was your community
And across that road
You sowed corn
And watered your cattle in that pan.

In years of dearth
We shared together
Helped each other in time of need.

Rest in peace, old man
Your kindred are here
Paying due respect
Rest in peace!

In Praise of the Shades

Chris Zithulele Mann

Hitching across a dusty plain last June,
down one of those deadstraight platteland roads,
I met a man with rolled-up khaki sleeves,
who told me his faults, and then his beliefs.
It's amazing, some people discuss more
with hitchhikers than even their friends.

His bakkie rattled a lot on the ruts,
so I'm not exactly sure what he said.
Anyway, when he'd talked about his church,

and when the world had changed from mealie-stalks
to sunflowers, which still looked green and firm,
he lowered his voice, and spoke about his shades.

This meant respect I think, not secrecy.
He said he'd always asked them to guide him,
and that, even in the city, they did.
He seemed to me a gentle balanced man,
and I was sorry to stick my kitbag
onto the road again and say goodbye.

When you are alone and brooding deeply,
do all your teachers and loved ones desert you?
Stand on a road when the fence is whistling.
You say, 'It's the wind', and if the dust swirls,
'Wind again', although you never see it.
The shades work like the wind, invisibly.

And they have always been our companions,
dressed in the flesh of the children they reared,
gossiping away from the books they left,
a throng who even in the strongest light
are whispering, 'You are not what you are,
remember us, then try to understand'.

They come like pilgrims from the hazy seas
which shimmer at the borders of a dream,
not such spirits that they can't be scolded, not such
mortals that they can be profaned,
for scolding them, we honour each other,
and honouring them, we perceive ourselves.

When all I ever hear about these days
is violence, injustice, and despair,
or worse than that, humourless theories
to rescue us all from our human plight,
those moments in a bakkie on a plain
make sunflowers from a waterless world.

Notes

platteland — Afrikaans: the countryside, literally 'flat-land' — large stretches of the
  South African countryside seem endlessly flat without the mountains that make
  other areas so majestic
bakkie — Afrikaans: small open truck or van

On Learning Sotho

Chris van Wyk

(for Isaac Sephoka)

I was a young Sotho boy then
a baby wetting a layette of words
and all of you laughed boisterously
when I swore at myself
not knowing the difference then
between 'nna' and 'wena'.
And I'd impress all the ladies
with 'dumela ausi!'
or 'moratiwa!' when I was randy.

The words crawled at first
no matter how they tried to walk
among the grown, bombastic men.
Oh I was a child again
joyfully sucking on the tits
of a language new to me
though it had always been
dangling invitingly from Agnes who makes the tea
or Mrs Mabuja who sweeps the office.

Thank you for your patience brother
and your English to guide my Sotho.
I'm growing now
and one day I will be as big as you
and Joseph and Walter and Lucky.
Then I will also laugh when you do
or cry
and understand why.

Notes
Sotho is the language-group most spoken in and around Johannesburg, containing,
    for instance, seSotho (as spoken in Lesotho) and Northern Sotho, saPedi and
    Southern Sotho (mainly spoken in the Transvaal).
nna — 1st person pronoun singular, 'I'
wena — 2nd person pronoun singular, 'you'
dumela ausi! — Hello, sister!
moraliwa — Loved one (Southern Sotho)

The next two poems reflect in different moods how unnecessary the awkwardnesses of separateness are:

I am the Man *from* No Baby Must Weep

Mongane Serote

i am the man you will never defeat
i will be the one to plague you
your children are cursed
if you walk this earth, where i too walk
and you tear my clothes and reach for my flesh
and tear my flesh to reach my blood
and you spill my blood to reach my bones
and you smash by bones and hope for my soul
the wind and the mountains and the stars
the sun the moon
saw you
i am the man you will never defeat
my song will merge with the breeze
my tears will freeze in time
you will walk the earth whose dust is my bones
and the sun will set like my eyes when they close for
the last time
and the moon will shine on my scream
i
i am the man you will never defeat
when the trees rattle you shall hear my last footsteps
this won't be your world
i am the man you will never defeat
i will be your shadow, to be with you always
and one day
when the sun rises
the shadows will move. heaving like a tired chest
there shall be millions of shadows
heaving
and the earth shall be cold
and the river will freeze
and the plants will refuse to grow
and the earth shall be dark
and the river shall be dark
and we will be alone

no man can defeat another man
we can sing together
make each other together
we can eat together
make the world together

no man can defeat another man.

Da Same, Da Same

Sipho Sepamla

I doesn't care of you black
I doesn't care of you white
I doesn't care of you India
I doesn't care of you clearlink
if sometimes you Saus Afrika
you gotta big terrible, terrible
somewheres in yourselves

I mean for sure now
all da peoples is make like God
an' da God I knows for sure
He make avarybudy wit' one heart

for sure now dis heart go-go da same
dats for meaning to say
one man no diflent to anader

so now
you see a big terrible terrible stand here
how one man make anader man feel
da pain de doesn't feel hisself
for sure now dats da whole point

sometime you wanna know how I meaning for
is simple
when da nail of say da t'orn tree
scratch little bit little bit of da skin
I doesn't care of say black
I doesn't care of say white
I doesn't care of say India

7

I doesn't care of say clearlink
I mean for sure da skin
only one t'ing come for sure
an' da one t'ing for sure is red blood
dats for sure da same, da same for avarybudy
so for sure now
you doesn't look anader man in de eye

Notes

Sepamla is telling the story of a Malawian cook in a Johannesburg work canteen
who talked of the strange ways of Southern Africans.

So long as you speak this poem aloud, you don't need a full word-for-word
translation.

of — if   *avarybudy* — everybody

clearlink — from the Afrikaans 'kleurling', a so-called Coloured person.

Points for discussion

● In BETWEEN OURSELVES does the image of the 'pit', the 'subsidence',
the 'gap' between these two people work well? As a result of that image
can you see how difficult it is for the people to interact? What do you
think the poet is implying by 'In the old days — fifty, a half dozen years
ago'? At the end of the poem, why does the poet use 'midnight' and why
'cry or cackle'?

● IN THE ACTUAL DIALOGUE what would you say the tone of the
poem is — is it one of accommodating another's viewpoint? or is it one of
reconciliation between people at odds? or is there a hint of menace in it?
Serote is one of the most powerful voices in Southern Africa: listen
carefully and hard to everything he says.

● In GRAVE OF UNKNOWN WHITEMAN what is the implication
contained in the words 'Your kindred are here'? Are you pleased to hear
the poet saying this? Or does he sound a bit like a sell-out to you?

● In IN PRAISE OF THE SHADES do you understand exactly what is
meant by the word 'shades' as it is used here? If you're not sure, look it up
in a dictionary. Has Mann conveyed his sense of respect and pleasure at
having another man share his beliefs with him strongly enough for you also
to feel it?

● What kind of a man does the poet emerge as in ON LEARNING
SOTHO?

● I AM THE MAN is an extract from a much longer poem. You can feel
how the poet uses repeated patterns of words or sentence structures for
cumulative effect. This is a feature of the much older 'izibongo' or praise-
poems of African oral literature.

● In what ways is Sepamla's device of using actual speech pronunciations
and rhythms in DA SAME, DA SAME effective? Is his argument a good
one? Can you counter it?

Some children growing up

In many ways Southern Africa is a marvellous place for young children to grow up in. In other ways, it's terribly exacting. Start with a story set in Zimbabwe:

The Mount of Moriah

Charles Mungoshi

In bed, in his room, Hama couldn't see them but he could clearly hear them behind the closed door in the sitting room.

'Or you could start afresh. Get a job and work harder,' Matura, the medicine man, was saying.

'I am not young anymore,' Hama's father said. 'These pains in my chest make it impossible for me to work or hope.'

'But you must have money to live on.'

'I know. That's why I am asking for your help. In the old days I wouldn't have bothered — I always had luck with the horses.'

'In the old days you had luck with everything. I never knew a man who had such luck as you had then.'

'But it's not there anymore now, is it? Lots of luck and no head with anything — money, women, jobs — everything — and today it's just as if I never had all that. One minute there — the next — gone.'

'You were a fool.' Pause. 'I have never met a bigger fool than you. You should have stayed married to one woman instead of taking them on and throwing them away the way you did — as if they were worn-out clothes you didn't need anymore.'

'I always felt that the women were finally more interested in my money than in me.'

'That was your trouble — and still is the trouble with you. Money.

9

You didn't care for anything else. Not even those women. I could mention two or three who really loved you but you never saw it.'

'They never gave me any children. I wanted children and all of them didn't care for children. They were just after my money.'

'You never wanted any children. They saw that much through you. Even the body in there – you have called him the result of an accident. No, children isn't what you wanted and they gave you none. That's why none of them stayed for very long with you.'

There was a long pause, then Hama heard his father croak: 'You have got to help me. Something is happening to me, I can feel it. If I don't have money soon I'll be vultures' meat!'

Matura's voice was very soft – touched with a kind of sadness when he answered:

'Why don't you go back to the reserve? Don't you have any relatives?'

'None of them care for me. They would rather see me dead first.'

'You can't blame them. It's you who has thrown them away. In the same way that you have thrown away some of the best of those women. No, you certainly can't lay the blame on them.'

'Don't rub it in. I know that only too well.'

'No you don't.'

There was another pause, then quite simply, Hama's father said: 'I need help now. You have got to help me.'

'And how do you think I can do that? I am not God. Only your own people can help you now.'

'At least you can bring back my luck. Bring back my luck so I can play the horses again.'

Matura took some time to answer, then he said: 'That's going to be difficult. You have played with your chances in the past and it's going to be very difficult for you to have them back again. You aren't the only one in the world, you know. Your ancestors gave you your time and you lost it, now it's other peoples' turn.'

'Are you saying that it can't be done?' There was despair in Hama's father's voice.

'Yes and no.' Silence then: 'I am saying that this time you have got to pay for every little scrap of luck that comes your way – with your own life. This time you have to make sacrifices. And only few people are capable of making sacrifices – you know. You are not one of them.'

'I will try. I would do anything to have my old luck back again.'

'Forget it. You don't know what you're talking about.

'I mean it.' It was almost a scream.

Matura laughed a nasty little laugh. He said: 'You don't have enough love to be able to make the sacrifice.'

'Love? What has love to do with it?'

'Everything. You see, you have got to sacrifice the thing you love beyond everything else to be able to bring back your luck. Now, what do you love beyond everything else? I bet you don't even love yourself!' Matura laughed again.

'My son . . .'

This time the medicine-man's laugh was really loud. He was enjoying himself. He said: 'Don't strain yourself. You don't love that boy. I have told you that already. You only feel that he is your responsibility. You crippled him, you can't get rid of the guilt so you think it's love. I think you even hate him!'

'How can you say that? He is the only one I have got!'

'We shall see about that.' Their voices were now very low.

In his room, Hama turned over and looked at the yellow wall, then through the window at the peach tree whose bare boughs pointed as if in prayer to the sky. The room was turning into a dungeon. Hama hardly remembered a day he had been out of it for more than half a day since he came back from the hospital without his left leg. And now he couldn't even remember how long back that was. He couldn't remember how long he had been in this hateful room with its flecking yellow walls and damp, rotting corners curtained off with spider netting studded with dead flies and cockroaches. He couldn't remember how long he had been fighting the bedbugs and the fleas and the lice and the other tiny things that gave him sleepless nights, biting, bloodsucking and irritating him. The fleas and the bugs and the lice were all right. At least he could see them. There were those other tiny things that he couldn't see, that he couldn't tell whether they were inside or outside him. Once he had tried to complain about them to his father and all he had got in answer was a very cold wordless look. Now he kept quiet. Even on the bad days when his father would come home complaining of how badly things were going with him, trying to trap Hama into talking, he would keep quiet. That had become a form of revenge on his father – and he could tell that his father hated him for it.

Hama was tired of his father. Most of the time he was only just indifferent to him. In the beginning he had cared: complaining that he wanted to go home to Aunt Rudo, that he couldn't sleep in this room or that the room needed cleaning – anything to attract his father's attention. But since his father never paid any attention to them, Hama had learned to forget that his father existed. Through all the time he had been living here with his father, Hama had been able to follow, at a long silent distance, his father's descent into the

11

mud — from one woman to another, though God knew how many friends with whom he always parted violenty and almost always at parties held in the house — quarrelling, fighting. And it was always over the same thing: these parasites were after his father's money, out to ruin him. Hama had slowly learned the cause of the friendships, the quarrels, the fights and the partings: money. 'My money' was a favourite phrase of his father's. He had heard it mentioned so much that even now, though he had never had any money himself, he violently hated what the word did to his ears: it was the sound of breaking crockery and furniture, of belching and vomiting, the stink of beer and stale vomit, the sound of a fist against a mouth so battered it sounded like a wet sponge — and blood all over the place. And the screams and the groans and the moans and the threats. He remembered too — from a very long hazy distance — and from constant reminders by his father — that it had been because of her incapability to use money properly that his mother had been sent away. Now he couldn't even remember how she had looked like. But he remembered her wet face. What he knew of her as a person he had got from his aunt, Rudo, where his father had sent him soon after the divorce. And any memories that Hama had of any time that he had ever been happy or talked at length to someone were of the time he had been staying with his aunt in the reserve. And he had cried and cried when his father came to take him away because it was time, his father had said, it was time that the boy went to school. It had just been a lie and Aunt Rudo had said it right there and then and he, Hama, had somehow known that is was just a plain old lie. Of course there hadn't been any school. Instead, there had been that terrible accident when his father drank while driving — drinking with that woman he had picked up in Enkeldoorn, telling her he had lots of money and that he was going to marry her. There had been no school: only that accident where the woman had died in hospital and Hama had lost his left leg. And his father had escaped with just a cut on his chin where the beard wouldn't grow now so that his father — who had loved to grow his beard long — sometimes using black shoe polish to keep it really black — had to shave it clean off because the scar always showed itself at its worst when he didn't shave. There had been that accident and those long dreary months in hospital with his leg hung above him in plaster before he came to live in this room which had slowly become worse than the hospital. Aunt Rudo had once paid him a visit but she hadn't stayed long because his father had been nasty to her and she had gone back home the same day and she had never come back. And since that time, Hama had not seen anyone from home. Talk had filtered in through that door to him — talk of how his father had cast away his own people and the curse that his mother had put on him. Whether this was true or not, Hama couldn't say. All he knew was that there were nights when his father shouted in his sleep, ranting and raving as if he were talking to someone who was bothering him; and that there were times when his father called in strange people — mostly medicine-men and women — to advise him on some matters.

And this evening was one of those times. And this time it looked worse because this was the fifth medicine-man his father had consulted in a row. In his room, Hama had been able to gather that his father had long lost his job, owed a lot of money to people and that the doctors had told him to stop smoking and drinking because he had contracted some disease that would kill him if he didn't listen to them. All this Hama heard without his meaning to hear it — like so many things he had heard since he had come to live here. But like some of those things, this had stuck in his mind without his meaning to let it stick.

They were talking loudly again in the sitting room.

'. . . a very big sacrifice,' the medicine-man was saying.

'I will try. What else can I do?'

'Only his heart, a piece of his liver, his genitals. Mix them with this . . .' And again the voices were too low for Hama to make out. But he knew what it was all about. He had heard lots like it. It was the good luck prescription. The medicine that his father wanted to be able to play the horses again. The medicine that his father needed to be rich once more. He had heard so many of these prescriptions in the past few weeks that he hardly paid any attention to what was being said right now. He was more interested in the scene that was taking shape of its own in his mind. He could see his father's yellow whiskers trembling and his tiny head bobbing up and down as if it were a gourd sitting on water, the yellow tobacco-stained talons digging into the wood of the table as visions of money, money and more money took possession of him till he just couldn't sit still, impatient to go out and try out this new medicine . . . Hama's heart tightened and he felt the little invisible insects inside him . . .

'Don't do it if you find you are afraid. You must be absolutely calm because one mistake might mean your death. I suggest that you see no woman, talk to no one, touch very little food before you perform the task. You must take care that no one sees you leave or come back. And you have to banish all worry from your mind. There is no turning back because once you do that — you are a dead donkey!' Then some inaudible words. Later, Hama heard them laughing. His father's laugh was very thin and nervous. Then the door to the street opened and shut. Hama's father stayed out very late that night and when he came back, Hama heard him talking to himself.

All that night, each time he woke up from his light sleep, Hama heard his father walking about in his bedroom, talking to himself.

*

Hama woke up when he heard his father's shuffling just outside his door. He mentally, without his being conscious of it, put on his armour. His father stopped and coughed, clearing his throat as if he had something very important to say. They were usually guilt-ridden requests to Hama to do something for him — little sedentary jobs like sewing some buttons on to his shirt or something of the sort. Hama never showed that he liked or disliked them.

His father coughed again and the door to Hama's room opened slightly. Hama looked away, pretending that he was asleep. His father came in and stood in his usual spot whenever he came into this room: close to the door as if ready to bolt out at the slightest hint of a threat on his life. He coughed again; that had become his way of saying good morning to his son.

'We are going home,' Hama's father said. For some time the statement hung embarrassingly naked in the air before Hama turned round to face his father. He fixed his eyes on his father.

'I have borrowed a car.' He took a step back from his son's staring eyes. His bloodshot eyes shifted off Hama's face and ricocheted off the boy's aluminium leg which Hama had thrust out of the blankets. His face twitched: 'This time there won't be any accident.' Hama looked away through the window at the peach tree. His father kept changing his weight from one leg to the other. Conversation with his son seemed to make him nervous. It was like climbing a very high mountain: he was a victim of vertigo. 'Don't you want to go home?'

Hama looked at his father silently and when he saw that he was about to repeat his question he said: 'Without your driver's licence?' His father's body jerked.

'Who told you?'

'I heard you talking to your friends in there.'

There was a painful silence, then Hama's father brought out a trembling hand and put it to his face. He turned away saying: 'Get yourself ready. I am going to bring the car round.' He almost slunk out of the room. Hama looked after him, wondering.

Since that time he came out of the hospital they had never gone home. Had Aunt Rudo died? The thought frightened the boy and he lay very still and all of a sudden he heard distant voices calling to each other at play in the village dusk. Aunt Rudo?

The door opened again and Hama felt his father's presence in the room.

'Is Aunt Rudo dead?' he asked without looking at his father.

His father looked at him furtively, surprised, unsettled and hurriedly left the room saying that nobody was dead and he had to buck up because it was a long drive home and they had to get there before duskfall.

They drove out of Harare along Beatrice Road. It was a close day, very still and already uncomfortably warm in the early morning.

In dead silence they slid through early morning shadows of tall gum trees along the road. Hama's father looked solemnly ahead, driving carefully, and Hama studied his father's tensed-up face in the rearview mirror. From his father's face, his eyes shifted to the grey road fanning out away from them, dappled with the shadows of departing night and the lights of coming day.

The sun climbed a little higher as they turned off the main road into a dusty easterly road. It was now hot and his father was sweating in his jacket. Hama resented him for not taking it off, because, by a weird association of thought he felt as if *he* was sweating and uncomfortable.

The lonely yellow road stretched before them in the scorching sun, so wide and so long that it gave Hama the illusion that they were not moving at all. Behind them the dust rose and hung in still clouds. The brittle grass and bushes beside the road were powdered yellow with dust and farther away from the road on both sides stretched plains of scattered trees and not much grass on the ground where the shadows of the trees were black blobs, cool and inviting. Looking at these dark patches of shadow, Hama felt comforted because he now felt as if he were sitting under one of those trees, in the shade out of the sun. He felt happy, and then, slowly, he began to feel sad because he smelled cattle and hay.

At Aunt Rudo's they were driving the cattle across the stream, bringing them home from the pastures in the dusty purple dusk singing 'The Mount of Moriah'. Aunt Rudo had taught him the song and had told him the story behind the song. Without actually singing it now, but with the tune going round and round inside him, he understood the song now better than that time long ago in the village. The length of the road — all that distance to be travelled — lent a kind of strange sadness — a sweet sadness — to the song. Moriah: a darkblue mountain in autumn haze across plains of dry

15

tall grass where the earth meets the sky. Abraham: long-bearded, broad-shouldered, in tattered coloured robes — he had seen a picture once when Aunt Rudo had taken him to church — mansmelling of snuff, fire, sweat, wet soil and the open air with a kindly wrinkled face and the wisdom of distant horizons in his eyes. Isaac: small, eager, smelling of goatmilk cream, his supple boy's back arched under the heavy burden of faggots: asking: 'But where is the lamb for the sacrifice, Father?' And Abraham's booming voice: 'God shall provide, son.' And, thinking about this, Hama imagined himself as Isaac, but when he looked in the rearview mirror and saw his father's mean, worry-strained face he felt betrayed. His father was a far cry from the self-confident, big-boned Abraham. And if his father couldn't be Abraham, then *he* was not Isaac ...

They were passing through a village, scattered here and there in the bush red-brick rondavels with thatched roof and an occasional glitter in the sun to show off somebody's big house with its corrugated iron roof, bare orange and white fields trembling with the heat of the sun, bordered with clumps of brown and yellow bush. And soon, this passed into dry grass plains, solitary, burdened with the heat, with an occasional acacia or *muhacha*, and always the illusion of water somewhere — this from the dark ripe-rapoko colour of the grass — but no water at all, until, all unexpectedly, the car dropped and they were crossing the brown-pebbled, sun-burned bed of a seasonal river, with, as the eye followed its course well-marked across the plain, a silver-fleck to show a stagnant pool of rust-coloured water, not any help for assuaging thirst. Further on, the plains had been burned. For many miles on either side nothing stood out in the thirstmaking shimmering blackness. 'The Mount of Moriah' died in the boy's mind and he grew silent and depressed. The road rose and fell, rose and fell again and again with the land as far as the eye could see and Hama smelled burning oil and felt the car rolling and shaking as if it would fall to pieces on the gravel of the road, ever so straight, so lonely, always and forever oppressed with the heat without any hope of any shade and he felt all the weight of the heat on him and it seemed to him as if they would never get anywhere and the sun would never stop burning and scorching everything black.

Then suddenly, the land broke up — gullies, a river: water!

His father stopped the car on the left side of the road and, in the sudden stillness of the world, with the roar of the car in their ears, they looked along the road they had come and ahead at the way they still had to go across the bridge. They were the only people in the whole world and this thought made Hama pity his father, and then ashamed to be ashamed of his father. His father pulled out the paper bag with their lunch and said: 'Let's find a cool place where we can sit.'

The grass-grown banks of the river were far back now from the water which flowed in a very thin trickle over a bed of pebbles.

Father and son walked slowly in the hot foot-sinking white sand along the river. There were tufts of water-gathered floatsam and river-dirt caught in the shrubs and boulders along the sand; and farther out from the banks, marking the extent of the floods that year. Half-buried in the sand and in the bed of the river Hama found some shells and up on the banks, in the trees, they surprised birds at sleep from the heat of the day.

They chose a water-polished rock in the shade of a *muonde* tree that grew on the very edge of a pool whose bottom they could not see. Water flowed smoothly and quietly round the rocks and boulders in the river and there were white bird-droppings on the rocks. It was very cool on the river. Hama leaned against the white and grey mottled bole of the tree and felt the tiredness leave him. It was as if that particular tree had been chosen in all the world for his back to lean on. A strange elation came upon him, but this turned into a sad melancholy when he looked at his father. The still day, the vastness of the blue sky and the strange loneliness of the river made him feel helpless. His father, too, looked very small − afraid of something both of them could feel but couldn't see.

All of a sudden, Hama was very afraid. 'We aren't going home to anyone's death, are we?' The lonely land, the river and the faraway sky forced him to talk in a whisper.

'I told you long back that we aren't going home to anyone's death and now just shut up, will you?' his father said. Hama felt that his father's agitation was not justified and something settled in him: an unknown fear. He felt, for the first time in his life, a deep need to appeal to someone for help. He saw his father's hands shaking as he tried to open the bag. The flesh on his face had become more wrinkled and his adam's apple was moving up and down as if he was having difficulty in swallowing something too big for his throat. His father now looked at the opposite bank of the river, very far away. Later, after some introductory coughs and shufflings in the bag, Hama heard him say:

'Feel hungry?'

The softness of the voice surprised Hama − and confused him. He didn't know whether the feeling of emptiness inside him was hunger or not. He nodded, though he didn't have any appetite for anything.

His father laid out several packages wrapped up in oil paper on the rock. He slowly began to unwrap them and laid out their lunch on the rock between them. There was bread cut into thin slices with wedges of cheese between the slices, pieces of biltong and two egg-rolls and a bottle of orange juice. They ate slowly, sipping in turn from the bottle, leaning against the tree. It was the first meal that Hama had ever had with his father and he couldn't enjoy it. He noticed that his father felt the same, too: he would take a timid bite on the bread, deliberate over-chewing it, then, not looking at the boy, his hand shaking, reach for the bottle of the juice, and when their fingers touched in passing the bottle both of them felt like saying 'Sorry' — then his father would swallow his food making a gurgle down his throat as if he were swallowing something hard and bitter, like medicine.

Then, all of a sudden, after the third bite on his second slice of bread, his father stood up and flung the unfinished piece of bread onto the water and walked a little way along the sand as if he were looking for something. Hama saw him wipe his forehead thrice and, there, dwarfed by the huge red bank, the white expanse of the heat-tormented sand and the great arid space above them, he looked forlornly small. Hama looked away and stared listlessly down the river at the smooth pebbles.

A bird screeched in the hot stillness and the boy nearly fell off the rock into the water. He had forgotten about the childhood stories of certain bird-cries that were portents of ill-omen. Now, the only bird of this type that he remembered was the owl. For two days an owl had cried on the roof of their house out in the reserve and Aunt Rudo hadn't said anything but he knew from the way her face fell that she felt that there was something bad that was going to happen. And there had been the accident.

And now, Hama wondered about this bird that had screeched up there in the trees on the bank. This bird wasn't an owl, he could tell that from its cry. Also, an owl was much bigger and slower in flight than this bird which he had not quite seen but only as a small fast dart against the glare of the sun above those trees on the bank. Maybe there was a bird fight up there. He saw some feathers dropping slowly down to the sand, descending in a spiral. The cry, so lonely, the black dart against the sun, and now the feathers — Hama felt afraid. But then the only other bird he knew that had the size of this other one was the honey-bird. The honey-bird was unpredictable. It could as easily lead you to a beehive as to a snake's nest. Hama shivered. He had once stepped on a coiled snake ... oh. He instinctively recoiled from the horror and as he leaned forward from the tree he felt a soft brush on his neck and he fell off the rock with a scream into the water. He had the hiccuping sensation of hitting cold water and the sudden desperate blacking-out feeling of sinking fast beyond all help, and then the relief — the shocked jolt of hitting a shallow bottom.

The water barely rose to his waist.

Crouching in the water, he had a glimpse of his father's horror-mottled face and in his trembling left hand a yellow scarf and in the right a big open knife . . . Then quickly, he felt himself being pulled up the chilly slimy face of the rock, his metal leg banging against the face of the rock as he went up. His father's face was twisted up painfully and his eyes jumped and his whiskers trembled as he said: 'All right? You aren't hurt are you?' And his father's hands all over his body, quick and agitated, feeling for any broken bones. He even touched the metal leg. Hama felt so embarrassed with this unusual nearness and attention of his father's that he couldn't look him in the face, his body tensed *away* from his father. Then he felt really bad when he discovered that his father's teeth were all black with rot — some, rusty-coloured — and they gave off a very sickening stench. An unbearable sadness washed over Hama. He said: 'You scared me!' His father said nothing. He kept on feeling here and there, jogging the boy's arm or leg this way and that, making such a short-breath fuss over him that for a moment Hama looked very closely, keenly, at his father, a new but short-lived fear taking a grip on him. This feeling disappeared as quickly as it had come and Hama felt hollow inside and now he was looking at his father and wondering what he wanted a yellow scarf and such a big knife for. His father caught him staring, and in a sudden burst of emotion, he hugged the boy so hard, his body shaking so violently that all the breath left Hama. His eyes were tightly shut. Hama's eyes were turned on the knife.

Yes. It was a big knife. Pocket-size, but still big. It evoked a strange fear in him and then something in him happened and he felt very, very sad for his father. The thought came to him that this knife was too big and clumsy to pare one's fingernails with — because it just came to him that must be what his father needed the knife for — to pare his fingernails with.

'Why didn't you ask me for a razor-blade?' Hama asked, suddenly wanting to help his father, fumbling in his wet pockets. He always kept bits of broken razor-blade in case he wanted to sharpen a stick to pick his teeth. It was a strangely pleasant sensation to lodge his tongue into some hollow in between his teeth and taste his own blood . . .

He found the blade and handed it to his father. Their eyes met. For a brief moment they both looked at the blade, then something violent seemed to happen inside his father. He closed his eyes tightly shut and with a pained cry grabbed the blade from the boy and flung it together with the knife far out across the water. Hama gasped as his eyes followed the course of the knife which flashed once in the sun and with a sad splash fell into the water, out of reach, of his life forever. He would have loved to own that knife . . . such a fine knife . . . He turned suddenly on his father and said: 'Why did you . . .?' His father slapped him hard across the cheek and then prevented his fall by quickly pulling him to himself and hugging him again, this time so tight that he let go when he heard Hama gasp in pain. Then his father was madly tearing the scarf into thin shreds and flinging them out into the water. His eyes didn't jump any more. They were narrowed on what he was doing. Hama was afraid. He turned away from his father to look at the pieces of cloth as they floated down the river. Then, behind him he heard big sobs. His father's head was dropped and he was crying into his hands. The first time to see his father crying, Hama was confused, then sad, then confused again and out of a need to appeal to someone — feeling very lonely and lost — he stretched out a hand and touched his father's hands which were cupped over his face. He tried to ply the fingers loose, to make his father uncover his face, and, finding the fingers too strong for him, he bit his lip, turned away and stared at the spot where the knife had fallen into the river. There was an itch in his nostrils, he felt them begin to flare, bit his lip harder — but there were tiny beady droplets in his eyes that split his vision into several bits — all complete in themselves — like seeing one image reflected in several mirrors — distorted. It was only by a very strong application of the will that he stopped the tears. Not a single drop touched his cheek. And his thoughts stayed on that one spot where the knife had 'died', re-creating the whirl-pools, following the path of the knife as it went down, he felt a calm come over him, a clean sad sort of joy that made him aware, almost physically — although he was't touching him — of the human presence of his father. But something told him that it wasn't yet time to look at his father, so, he kept on looking down the river. Caught in a cleft made by two rocks, dancing slowly in the current, Hama saw the piece of bread his father had thrown away.

'Let's go,' his father said. Slowly Hama turned and saw his father's hand in mid-motion to touching his shoulder. He saw the hand drop, but the face took a longer time turning the other way. His father's eyes didn't jump much anymore, although they seemed to be looking into a very, very long distance.

*

They walked back to the car and the boy felt the warm trickles of water coursing down his back from his hair.

His father turned the car's nose back the way they had come.

'We aren't going home?'

'Oh, yes we are!' his father said. But they were driving to Salisbury. Hama looked at his father. His father noticed it and making a large sweep of the land they were driving in, with his eyes, he said: 'My father — your grandfather — that is, used to spend days and days hunting in this area. This was before he settled where we are settled now. He was running away from some people — some enemies. Our home is really beyond those mountains.' For a brief second, his father's eyes rested on him, then they were looking at the land again. Finally they came to rest on the road ahead of them. Hama couldn't think of anything to say to this, so he kept quiet. The sun was almost down, not yet but going down, and his father's eyes were narrow points of light that distantly reflected the long road as it fanned into them. His father's eyes didn't jump about anymore.

'Think we can make it before sundown?' his father asked. 'I used to, you know, when you were still a baby and I was driving for Makombe — but then that was a bus and it could take the punishment on these roads. Now, a small car like this — but, still, let's see ...'

Then, all of a sudden, Hama lost the sound of the engine ... only the rush of the cool wind and the roll of the wheels sitting firmly on the road. And all the way to Salisbury Hama listened to the roar of the car and his father's voice above the roar, relating what had happened in that dark time long ago before Hama had been born or was still a baby.

Note

At the time of writing, Zimbabwe was known as Southern Rhodesia. Present day Harare was then called Salisbury. The Harare referred to in the story was a township on the outskirts of Salisbury.

Growing up in a town or city is very different. The children in the next two pieces grew up in black urban townships, while the third piece is set in what was then a pretty 'mixed' area, of 'poor whites', 'Coloured' people and Indian people.

Boy on a Swing

Mbuyiseni Oswald Mtshali

Slowly he moves
to and fro, to and fro,
then faster and faster
he swishes up and down.

His blue shirt
billows in the breeze
like a tattered kite.

The world whirls by:
east becomes west,
north turns to south;
the four cardinal points
meet in his head.

Mother!
Where did I come from?
When will I wear long trousers?
Why was my father jailed?

One Small Boy Longs for Summer

Mafika Gwala

(*for Bill Nanghton*)

The kettle hisses
Mother moves about the kitchen
sliding from corner to corner.
The fire from the stove
pierces into the marrow.
And mother pushing towards the stove
warns of the steam.
My young brother, Thamu, jerks my arm
violently: Stop leaning on me, your elbow
has sunk into my thigh.

Apology
> I wasn't aware.

The kettle sings
> Some distant far-away song?

Mother picks it up
with an almost tender care.
Sets me thinking of a war-picture
The actor carefully setting the charge
and smiling all the time
> I'll also be a soldier

when I'm old — why, Uncle Shoba was one.
Father drops the paper on the table
He comes to join us
> — staring coldly round.

It's no frown really,
But he's grinding his jaws.
> Maybe it's the July

Handicap.

The kettle purrs now
Steam is escaping; it kisses the ceiling
and vanishes, Mother is pouring the violent waters
into the coffee-jug. Coffee.
Yes, I need some coffee — a mug of hot coffee.
Very rousing.
We can't play outside — I must not go, I know.
> How we danced in the rain. We are so tired

of the winter: It's so dingy outside.
We can't play inside — I'm so tied up.
It's so boring, I feel like bursting into
a cracking laughter; but father,
he'll go mad.
It's so steamy inside
I feel I could bite the walls down.
If only it makes the winter pass.

Notes
the July Handicap — the Durban July, the country's premier horse-racing
event.

23

Gerty's Brother

Ahmed Essop

I first saw Gerty in a shop in Vrededorp. Vrededorp, as everyone knows, is cleft in two by Delarey Street: on the one side it is colonized by us blacks and on the other side by whites. The whites come over to our side when they want to do their shopping, and return with a spurious bargain or two. I saw her in a shop in the garishly decorated Indian shopping lane called Fourteenth Street. I had gone there with my friend Hussein who wanted to see a shop-keeper friend of his. I think the shop was called Dior Fashions, but of that I am not quite sure because shop follows shop there and this one didn't strike me as being in any way fashionable. Anyway, that is where I saw her. My friend spoke to the shopkeeper — a fat dark man with a darker moustache — and I just looked around and smoked a cigarette.

I sat down on a chair and then I noticed two figures darken the doorway and enter the shop, a girl and a boy. The shopkeeper spoke to the girl and then suddenly laughed. She laughed too, I think. I wouldn't have taken any further notice of the group as I was seated at the back of the shop. But then the shopkeeper switched to Gujarati and spoke to my friend. I heard him say that she was easy and would not give much trouble in removing her undergarments to anyone, but one had to be careful as there was the usual risk involved. Hussein replied that he was keen and wouldn't like to waste much time about the matter. I think the shopkeeper introduced him to her at this stage. Then I heard him telling Hussein that he was going to organize a dance at his place on the following Saturday evening, that he was going to invite Gerty, and that if Hussein was interested he could take her away from his place. All this he said in Gujarati, rather coarsely I thought.

Later, when Hussein and I had climbed into his Volkswagen and were on our way to Fordsburg, he informed me that to soften her before the party on Saturday he had bought the girl a frock. He asked me how I liked her and I said she was all right as far as I was concerned, though, of course, I had not been near enough to see her properly and size her up. But I said she was all right and he felt very satisfied at having bumped into a white girl. He told me that she lived in Vrededorp, 'on the other side', and that she seemed to be very easy. He said that when he had done with her he would

24

throw her over to me and I could have her as well. I answered with a vague 'Let the time come'. He then said something about 'pillar to post', and laughed as the car tore its way through the traffic into Fordsburg.

Saturday night I was at my landlady's, stripped to the waist because of the heat, reading an old issue of *The New Statesman*. There was a knock on the door and somebody asked for me and entered. It was Hussein all dressed up with bow tie and cuff-links and gleaming shoes that were out of place in my spartan room.

'Where to, my dandy friend?' I asked admiringly.

'To the dance party. I thought you would be ready. You promised to come with me.'

I said I had forgotten, but that I would be ready in a minute. I dressed quickly, but didn't care to put on a white shirt or a tie. I wasn't very particular about what I wore and I think it pleased my friend because my appearance was something of a foil to his, and set off to advantage his carefully put-together looks.

We set off in his Volkswagen for Vrededorp and in a few minutes the car braked sharply in Eleventh Street in front of the house of Hussein's shopkeeper friend. We were quite early and there were not many people present. Hussein's friend was happy to see us and he introduced us to those who were there. There were some lovely-looking girls in shimmering coral and amber and amethyst-coloured saris and others in more sober evening dresses.

After a while Hussein asked to see the shopkeeper privately, and I think they went out to the front verandah of the house. When they returned I saw that Hussein was not too pleased about something or other. Other girls arrived, all gaily dressed and very chic and charming and I was beginning to look forward to a swinging evening. The girls offered me tea and cake and other tasty things to eat and I didn't refuse as my boarding-house wasn't exactly a liberal establishment. All this time my friend Hussein was walking in and out of the room, and was on the look-out whenever someone knocked on the door and entered the house. The party got going and we danced, ate the refreshments provided and talked some euphonious nonsense.

I was just getting interested in a girl, when my friend interrupted me and said that he wanted to see me urgently. I followed him and we went to the verandah. Someone had switched off the lights and I saw two figures standing there, a girl and a small boy. He introduce her to me as Gerty. He then took me aside and asked me if I could drive the two of them to the Zoo Lake immediately and leave them in the park for a while, and if I could keep her brother company while he saw to Gerty's needs. As it was a risky business he didn't want the others in the party to know. He would like to get done with it before joining the party.

I said I didn't mind and the four of us got into the car. I drove to the Lake. It was a lovely night in December and we breathed in the luminous wind of the city streets as the car sped along. Hussein and Gerty sat in the back seat. They didn't say much to each other, but I guessed that they were holding hands and fondling. Gerty's brother sat beside me. He must have been seven or eight, but I didn't take much notice of him. He was eating some cakes and chocolates that Hussein had taken from the house. I dropped the pair in a park near the Lake. Hussein asked me to return in about an hour's time. The park was a darkness of trees and lawns and flowers, and it occurred to me that it made no difference if one slept with a white or a black girl there.

Gerty told her brother that he mustn't worry and that she was all right and that he should go with me for a while. Before I drove off he asked me what they were going to do and I said they must be a bit tired and wanted to rest, but that did not sound convincing. Then I said that they had something to discuss in private and the best place was in the park. He agreed with me and I started the car. I didn't feel like driving aimlessly about for an hour so I drove towards the lake. I asked the boy what his name was and he said Riekie.

I parked the car under some pine trees near a brightly-lit restaurant. There were people dining on the terrace amid blaring music, others were strolling on the lawns or resting on the benches. I asked Riekie if he would like an ice-cream and took him to the restaurant and bought him one. We went down to the water's edge. The lake is small with an islet in the middle; a fountain spouted water into shifting rays of variegated light. Riekie was fascinated by it all and asked me several questions.

I asked him if he had ever sat in a boat. He said he hadn't. I took him to the boat-house and hired one. The white attendant looked at me for a moment and then at Riekie. I knew what he was thinking about but I said nothing. He went towards the landing-stage and pointed to a boat. I told Riekie to jump in, but he hesitated. So I lifted him and put him into the boat. He was light in weight and I felt the ribs under his arms. A sensation of tenderness for the boy went through me. You must understand that this was the first time I had ever picked up a white child.

I rowed out towards the middle of the lake, and went around the fountain of kaleidoscopic lights. Riekie was gripped by wonder. He trailed his hands in the cool water smelling of rotted weeds, and tried to grab the overhanging branches of the willows along the banks.

It was time to pick up Hussein and Gerty. Riekie looked disappointed, but I said I would bring him there again. At this he seemed satisfied and I rowed towards the landing-stage.

Hussein and Gerty were waiting for us. They got into the car and we returned to the party in Eleventh Street.

The party was now in full swing. There were many girls and I didn't waste much time. My friend stuck to Gerty, and if he was not dancing with her he was talking to her. And by the time the party ended at midnight Riekie had fallen asleep on a sofa and had to be doused with water to wake him.

We dropped Gerty and her brother at a street corner on our way to Fordsburg. Hussein had rooms of his own in Park Road, situated in a small yard at the end of a passage. A tall iron gate barred the entrance to the passage. There were only three rooms in the yard. Hussein occupied two and the other was occupied by a decrepit pensioner who lived in his room like some caged animal, except that no one ever came to see him.

At first Hussein was afraid to tell Gerty where he lived. There was the usual risk involved. But I think eventually he came to the conclusion that in life certain risks had to be taken if one was to live at all. And so Gerty and her brother came to his rooms and she took on the role of mistress and domestic servant and Riekie became the pageboy.

Gerty and Riekie were very fond of each other. The harsh realities of life − they were orphans and lived in poverty with an alcoholic elder brother − had entwined them. Hussein didn't mind Riekie's presence. In fact the boy attached himself to him. My friend was generous, and besides providing Gerty with frocks for summer, he bought the boy clothing and several pairs of shoes. Riekie was obedient and always ready to run to the shops for Hussein, to polish his shoes or wash the car. In time his cheeks began to take on colour and he began to look quite handsome. I noticed that he wasn't interested in boys of his own age; his attachment to his sister seemed to satisfy him.

Riekie would often come to my landlady's in the company of Hussein, or my friend would leave him there when he had some business with Gerty. If I was in the mood to go to the movies I would take him with me.

And then things took a different turn. Hussein came to understand that the police had an eye on him, that somehow they had come to know of Gerty and were waiting for an opportunity to arrest him in incriminating circumstances. Someone had seen a car parked for several nights near his rooms and noticed the movements of suspicious-looking persons. And he was convinced the police were after him when one night, returning home late, he saw a man examining the lock of the gate. As he was not in the mood for a spell of prison, he told her that she should keep away from him for some time, and that he would see her again as soon as things were clear. But I think both of them realised that there wasn't much chance of that.

There wasn't much that one could tell Riekie about the end of the affair. My friend left it to Gerty, and went to Durban to attend to his late father's affairs.

One Sunday morning I was on my way to post some letters and when I turned the corner in Park Road there was Riekie, standing beside the iron gate that led to my friend's rooms. He was clutching two bars with his hands, and shouting for Hussein. I stood and watched as he shouted. His voice was bewildered.

The ugly animal living in the yard lurched out of his room and croaked: 'Goh way boy, goh way white boy. No Hussein here. Goh way.'

Riekie shook the barred gate and called for Hussein over and over again, and his voice was smothered by the croaks of the old man.

I stood at the corner of the street, in my hand the two letters I intended to post, and I felt again the child's body as I lifted him and put him into the boat many nights ago, a child's body in my arms embraced by the beauty of the night on the lake, and I returned to my landlady's with the hackles of revolt rising within me.

How different are the lifestyles of the white children in the next two pieces — from that of Gerty's brother, from those of the black children and from one another's:

In the House of the Father

Jeni Couzyn

Christmas, the turning time, the final reckoning and the forgiveness, we rode towards each year, over humps of bitterness, towards the father

omnipotent and bountiful night rider with his magical
reindeer and sack full of gifts −
you could rely on him always to be there when you got there

accept the culmination of your year in his lap
hear all, forgive with a wish, and let you
begin all over;

a time of reprieve and new resolutions, time when you could
believe in new beginnings, a time of peace and long
playtime. With a hand in the dark

it began before dawn. The sun would rise over the city
as we passed the last gold hills of the mine dumps. Always
I saw children leaping up them, and in my head, in golden depths

a heap of little skeletons. Then the long hot hours dreaming
through the dorps each its single tree and tin roofs blazing
each its lone dog barking and black silent men

propped on the verandah of the general store, drinking
lemonade. Endless car games, the singing game chanting every
   rhyme we knew
from ten green bottles to jesus loves me over the veld

to pass the time. At last, crossing, purple and lonely
the valley of a thousand hills, the tropical
deep smell of heavy flowers would glut the evening

and my father offered sixpence for the first to see the sea.
And there it was after a sudden unbending − that immense blue
   promise.
Then inland into the sugar cane in the deep of night

The rustle of dunes and the sugar cane fields
the farmers who kept pythons fifty feet long to keep the rats down
and at midnight

the cottage. O the damp smell of foliage, smell of salt
and the seas's heavy breathing in the night, stray cries
of live things, batswing, shadow, sleep, and a ring of mornings.

The snakes were the price. In their hundreds they inhabited
our world at christmas. They were the hazard
in the garden. And they were everywhere

tangled in undergrowth. slithering over your feet in the pathway
stretched across doorways in the sun
lurking under the banana plant and nesting in the luckybean tree

they were everywhere, everywhere. And happiness was everywhere
in the father's time, who came down from heaven
in his red dressing gown and my father's shoes at the appointed time

cottonwool beard lobsided across his grin
his arms full of parcels.
His was the future that always came, keeping its promise.

In the house of the father the year would turn
a flower full blown, shedding its petals.
Glistened in your hand a free gift, a clean seed.

Notes
dorp — Afrikaans: small country town

Next time

Sheila Roberts

My eyeballs ache in the white light as I step outside. I pinch them
tightly to stop the pain and sit down on the red-polished stoep. I
hate Sunday; it's too quiet. It seems the sun comes down closer to
the ground and burns hotter because the usual noise is not holding it
back. It is so still. If it had been this quiet last night, I would not
need to press my head in my fingers. I would not have cried. But he
screamed and sang and stamped. *Here*, I hate him. Next time I shall
hit him; true as God. I shall hit him. I hate Sunday. I can hear her
strike another match. I know her hands are shaking again.

I slit my eyes and make out the iron shack across the road. It
shines. It is talking to the sun. The leaves on our kaalgatperske tree
are just old pieces of rag. I know their feel, sort of coolish and soft.
You crush them until the green juice runs under your finger nails. It
tastes gal but the peaches are tight and sweet. That zizz must be a

30

buzz-bike. I wonder if it is Piet. I open my eyes a bit wider so that the stones of the path show one-one from out of the hot grey colour I see when my eyes slit.

I have got a week to find myself a strong kierie so that next time I can hit him. Just on the side of his head. Not too hard. Then he will be out and be quiet so that we can sleep. I would not kill him but I would not care if he was dead.

If it was not Sunday I could go to school. I hate Sunday. Only Jan knows about him at school, but then only Jan and me in the class come from the camp. In my uniform I am the same as the others. There is no difference and they are not better than me. He cannot sing and scream there. When he does it in that loud way I have to bite my teeth together or I will grab his face with my hands. He can never come there. When old Doef asked me how I hurt my hand I said in the scrum because I could not say I hit the wall when he started to piss in the kitchen and I knew she would wipe it. If I said I hit the wall the ous would laugh.

Tubby is scratching. I see him under the house in the brown shade. He looks funny with his leg stuck up and his neck stretched out while he scratches quick and rough. His eyes bulge as if he was liking it. I would get under the house too if I could but it only stands maybe eighteen inches off the ground. All the houses in this military camp are like that. Prefab is the name. I don't like to look at them because they are all the same. If they were people they would be ashamed I think. I like to look the same as the boys in my class but I am not the same as them inside myself. I would be ashamed to be the same even as Jan. Jan did not spot the akkedis on the stone when we went past in Petrus's 'Valiant'. He can't notice things. He laughed when we went to the abattoirs and I told him the osse smell their death. But I could see. Ag stupid I said to him. Why don't the army make these houses all different I think. If I was the one to say I would order each one to be different. Maybe then there would not be drinking because the men would be ashamed to be the same when the houses are different. No he would drink. Even if you put him in a snob hotel he would drink.

Come and have your breakfast Mikey she calls me. My head is sore. Mikey she calls. Then I hear him cough and draw the phelgm up noisily so I do not move. How I hate his guts. Come and eat Mikey. I have to go in but I won't look at him. I will make as if he is dead. It is dark inside after the bright sun but I feel for my chair and reach for the salt for my eggs and I hear him say in a slow begging voice Anna get me a regmaker. No Bill man it will start you off again. Have some more black coffee. But I am sick. Well regmakers

31

won't make you better. We have not slept she says and her voice is like sand scraped on a stone. We have not slept. As if he would care. Get me a regmaker Anna. I have to look at him because my eyes look up without me but I hold my neck down. He is flabby and an ugly grey colour except for the veins on his cheeks and in his eyes. They are blue-red. His skin hangs and his grey beard is like a worndown brush. His grey hair is wet with the sweat but still it sticks up because he has been putting his fingers through it. His chest hangs like soft tits in his vest. He is pap. I could easily hit him. I could kill him if I wanted to. I know she will get him the regmaker because she always does whatever he says. That is why I must hit him next time. She will never stand up to him but only sink down more and more and smoke and smoke until the tiredness finishes her. But I will fix him next time.

I finish my eggs without speaking and swallow my coffee in big swallows. I must get outside because the stink of stale brandy and piss and old stompies will not let me breathe and the sides of my head are too tight. I hear Jan whistle at the gate and push my chair back. Take your hat Mikey she says or you will burn red but her voice is tired and she knows of course I will not take my hat. I couldn't care that the ous call me rooinek and sometimes white rat because of my hair and face. At least I am not a hairyback I tell them. I will go with Jan to the river and he can fish while I sleep or maybe I will find a good strong dry branch there.

*

You are no example for a boy I said Bill you want him to have a better chance in life than us and he's not stupid he's young for his class look at the way he fixes the plugs and changes the elements for me and he doesn't run around nights like the others his age you should be more of a father and give up the drink I said but he doesn't listen to me let him go if he doesn't like it he says sis on you Bill he's only fifteen and the spitting image of you as a kid so he says so what at fifteen I was earning money yes and look what habits you picked up on the mines habits what habits well the drink you're ruining your health I said do you want to start on that again the old old story he says with that look on his face so I shut up but it's no home for a boy what could I do I couldn't leave and maybe not be able to support my own child I hate him he said last night when he saw him unbutton his fly in the kitchen and I hate him and he cried but I held him so he could not hit the wall like the last time I hate him he's your father Mikey I said honour thy so he asked me so do you expect me to love a pig like him he's not my father then he cried with his face all screwed up and his sobs hoarse I have not

32

seen him cry in years ag it's his nerves mine are gone too but I must maar keep the peace then the thumping against the headboard and the old war songs horsie keep your tail up and if you were the only girl but the groans and shouts are the worst it must have been three o'clock it's a wonder he doesn't hurt himself when he falls off try to sleep dear I said but he cried and cried then put his pillow on his head next time he said next time Jan is his best friend but old van der Watt also pots so he can't sleep there I suppose in a year or so he will be out all night with girls so why.

*

It is so nice and cool and humming at the river. Cool as peace. In peace there is no crying. I dip my hair in the water and feel the cold against my head. You will frighten the fish says Jan. I lie back. The world is spinning I know I say to Jan because if you look up like this at the sky through the leaves you can see the clouds moving along and you know it feels like moving. And you know Jan I say there where the leaves are thick the blue sky looks like a jigsaw puzzle. Shoesh says Jan because he wants a fish to bite. I walk off to let him have peace and quiet. I like Jan because he is also English. We are the only two English ous in the school. *Here* look at this I say to myself when I see the stick. Tubby starts to run when I pick it up; he thinks I am going to throw it for him to get, but I don't throw it, I just balance it in my hands. How long do you reckon this is Jan I ask him when I get back. Maybe two foot he says. I bet it weighs a lot I say. If I hit you with this I could kill you I say especially if it lands across your neck. Just try and I'll donder you says Jan and resets his hook. I take out my pocket knife and start to smooth it. What do you want with that stick says Jan. Nothing. Well throw it away. No jong I am going to keep it. When I get home I am going to drop it through my window in case he sees it I think.

I wish you would stop bawling Ma I shout at her. At least he's quiet now. Now we can sleep. I told you next time I would hit him. You hit your own father she says and puts the wet cloth on his head. So what; he is not my father. Leave him I tell her and go to sleep. I am going to hit him every time when he starts that screaming. She starts to put her coat on over her night-dress. I must go and find Doctor Steyn she says. Go to sleep. Ma I tell her grabbing her coat but she looks so scared I leave her. She runs out.

I sit by the bed and look at him. I will not mind it if you are dead I whisper to him. His lips have a white crust on them of old frothy spit and his bottom false teeth sag out a little. He used to stick them out at me just like that to tease me when I was small. His head looks very small to me. His hair is cut very short on the sides like all the army chaps. I put my hand close to his face but I cannot tell if he is breathing. I cannot make myself touch him so I don't know if he is warm.

He is lying so quietly now. You should have kept quiet like this every Saturday I tell him, then you would not have got hit. She always says he is a clever man. An intelligent man. Clever for what I ask. Just clever for bragging. He always starts by bragging. Then comes the singing. No she says if it wasn't for the depression and the war he could have made something of himself. Why can't he make something of himself now I ask except a dronklap. It is in his blood from the years in Italy she says but Lukas's father was also in Italy and he has the garage business. He doesn't pot. We all have our faults she says. So I ask so must I like him for being a soak. Then she says words to me from the Bible about honouring thy father. Bull I say that's all bull.

I can hear footsteps along the path. She is coming back with someone. It's probably Captain Steyn. I stand up quickly when I hear her say this way Doctor. One point of her night-dress is dirty where it hang out of her coat and drags on the floor. Doctor Steyn nods friendly at me. He knows me well. He took out my tonsils when I was eight. That was before we came to this camp. I was sorry that time because he was there in the ward and he fell off the chair he was so drunk. Captain Steyn helped him. He told him say goodbye to young Mike here; visiting hours are over but they weren't really.

Captain Steyn bends over the bed and starts examining him. I had better get him to the hospital he says. What exactly happened, did you say, he says straightening himself. My throat is closing and my heart pushes against my ribs. I want to ask if he is dead.

Doctor there was a crash, she says. I ran in and there he was lying on the floor. He must have hit his head. He often falls off the bed when in this state. She is talking in her best voice.

And do you two lift him onto it again he asks.

Yes Doctor.

I see. Well I shall telephone for the ambulance from the Orderly Room. You will probably want to go along to the hospital with your husband, so get yourself dressed quickly. He pats her shoulder.

Thank you Doctor.

He leaves the room and I run after him. He moves so fast I only catch up with him on the stoep. Captain Steyn I say Captain Steyn. He does not stop walking so I follow him to the gate. Captain Steyn I say Captain Steyn he did not fall. I hit him with a strong stick I found at the river. It was when he started singing and groaning. I

34

said true as God I would do it if he did not let us sleep this time.

Did your mother see you he asks slowly. Yes Captain Steyn but she could not stop me.

Well well. He thinks and looks at me. I am sorry my pyjamas are torn across the knees. Did you stop to think what would have happened to you had you killed him he asks.

No Captain Steyn but he has got to let us sleep I say. He looks at me again as if he wanted to remember all about me.

Well my boy he says if I were you I would not tell anyone. I like his eyes and his sad sort of way of looking so I nod okay.

The ambulance is standing at the gate now. They have put him inside on a stretcher and now they are helping her inside. I am going to wait here on the stoep. It is cool and the leaves of the peach tree flap and rub against each other as if they are telling secrets. Tubby is lying with his jaw on my foot. Her old flowerbeds are like a soft smell resting on the air. I can hear loud voices coming from the mess across the way and hammering music from the Venter's house over the road. I put my fingers in my ears and look up. It would be nice to be deaf I think. I can still hear the music like it is under the sea. It would be nice to be completely deaf because then I could just shut my eyes when I wanted to. If you shut your eyes you can't see nothing not like when you shut your ears. The stars look clean. I think to myself Mikey you are on a huge ball. Its name is earth and you are rolling among stars. On this ball earth there is grass and rivers and peaches and a brakkie but no people. No there is another boy named Jan but he is sleeping now.

Notes

Here — Afrikaans: Lord! It is a two-syllabled word, roughly 'hear-ra'. Also 'Heer'

Kaalgatperske — Afrikaans: nectarine, literally 'bare-bum-peach'.

gal — Afrikaans: bitter

kierie — Afrikaans: 'a fighting club or stick usually with a knobbed head' (Branford Dictionary); also 'knobkierie' or 'knobkerrie'

ous — Afrikaans: plural for 'chap', 'fellow'

akkedis — Afrikaans: lizard

osse — Afrikaans: oxen

regmaker — Afrikaans: a 'put me right', another drink

pap — Afrikaans: flabby

stompies — Afrikaans: cigarette-ends

rooinek — Afrikaans: literally 'a red neck', a derogatory term for an Englishman

hairyback — a derogatory term for an Afrikaner

donder — Afrikaans: to hit, to beat up

jong — Afrikaans: literally 'young' but used colloquially as one uses 'man' or 'mate'

dronklap — Afrikaans: drunkard

brakkie — Afrikaans: a small mongrel dog

Points for Discussion

• The story of Abraham and Isaac is obviously central to what happens in Mungoshi's story, THE MOUNT OF MORIAH. How well is it integrated into the story main story? What's your feeling about the end of the story? Is Hama's life going to change?

• Only the last line of BOY ON A SWING fixes it in time and place as South African: until then it could have been any boy living anywhere. True or false?

• Clearly, ONE SMALL BOY LONGS FOR SUMMER is a catalogue of a boy's various winter discontents. But what is the tone? Do you feel any bitterness? Is it even affectionate?

• In GERTY'S BROTHER think how remarkable it is that the young man who narrates the story should say: 'You must understand that this was the first time I had ever picked up a white child.' What must he have felt at that moment? And what lies behind the final words of the story: '. . . with the hackles of revolt rising within me'?

• How entirely different is the child's world in Jeni Couzyn's IN THE HOUSE OF THE FATHER! 'Happiness was everywhere', she says. What else was there in this girl's life each Christmas holiday?

• Did you expect that Mikey would hit his father in NEXT TIME, or did it come as a surprise? What do you think about Dr Steyn's reaction? Did you find it easy to jump from one narrator to another? Does the lack of punctuation in the section of the mother's thoughts work for you?

In the Country

It is the varied experiences and the different kinds of 'country' that these next pieces want to reflect:

The Bridegroom

Nadine Gordimer

He came into his road camp that afternoon for the last time. It was neater than any house would ever be; the sand raked smooth in the clearing, the water drums under the tarpaulin, the flaps of his tent closed against the heat. Thirty yards away a black woman knelt, pounding mealies, and two or three children, grey with Kalahari dust, played with a skinny dog. Their shrillness was no more than a bird's piping in the great spaces in which the camp was lost.

Inside his tent, something of the chill of the night before always remained, stale but cool, like the air of a church. There was his iron bed, with its clean pillowcase and big kaross. There was his table, his folding chair with the red canvas seat, and the chest in which his clothes were put away. Standing on the chest was the alarm clock that woke him at five every morning and the photograph of the seventeen-year-old girl from Francistown whom he was going to marry. They had been there a long time, the girl and the alarm clock; in the morning when he opened his eyes, in the afternoon when he came off the job. But now this was the last time. He was leaving for Francistown in the Roads Department ten-tonner, in the morning; when he came back, the next week, he would be married and he would have with him the girl, and the caravan which the department provided for married men. He had his eye on her as he sat down on the bed and took off his boots; the smiling girl was like

37

one of those faces cut out of a magazine. He began to shed his working overalls, a rind of khaki stiff with dust that held his shape as he discarded it, and he called, easily and softly, '*Ou Piet, ek wag.*' But the bony black man with his eyebrows raised like a clown's, in effort, and his bare feet shuffling under the weight, was already at the tent with a tin bath in which hot water made a twanging tune as it slopped from side to side.

When he had washed and put on a clean khaki shirt and a pair of worn grey trousers, and streaked back his hair with sweet-smelling pomade, he stepped out of his tent just as the lid of the horizon closed on the bloody eye of the sun. It was winter and the sun set shortly after five; the grey sand turned a fading pink, the low thorn scrub gave out spreading stains of lilac shadow that presently all ran together; then the surface of the desert showed pocked and pored, for a minute or two, like the surface of the moon through a telescope, while the sky remained light over the darkened earth and the clean crystal pebble of the evening star shone. The campfires — his own and the black men's, over there — changed from near-invisible flickers of liquid colour to brilliant focuses of leaping tongues of light; it was dark. Every evening he sat like this through the short ceremony of the closing of the day, 'slowly filling his pipe, slowly easing his back round to the fire, yawning off the stiffness of his labour. Suddenly he gave a smothered giggle, to himself, of excitement. Her existence became real to him; he saw the face of the photograph, posed against a caravan door. He got up and began to pace about the camp, alert to promise. He kicked a log farther into the fire, he called an order to Piet, he walked up towards the tent and then changed his mind and strolled away again. In their own encampment at the edge of his, the road gang had taken up the exchange of laughing, talking, yelling, and arguing that never failed them when their work was done. Black arms gestured under a thick foam of white soap, there was a gasp and splutter as a head broke the cold force of a bucketful of water, the gleaming bellies of iron cooking pots were carried here and there in the talkative preparation of food. He did not understand much of what they were saying — he knew just enough Tswana to give them his orders, with help from Piet and one or two others who understood his own tongue, Afrikaans — but the sound of their voices belonged to this time of evening. One of the babies who always cried was keeping up a thin, ignored wail; the naked children were playing the chasing game that made the dog bark. He came back and sat down again at the fire, to finish his pipe.

After a certain interval (it was exact, though it was not timed by a watch, but by long habit that had established the appropriate lapse of time between his bath, his pipe, and his food) he called out, in Afrikaans, 'Have you forgotten my dinner, man?'

From across the patch of distorted darkness where the light of the two fires did not meet, but flung wobbling shapes and opaque, overlapping radiances, came the hoarse, protesting laugh that was, better than the tribute to a new joke, the pleasure in constancy to an old one.

Then a few minutes later: 'Piet! I suppose you've burned everything, eh?'

'*Baas*?'

'Where's the food, man?'

In his own time the black man appeared with the folding table and an oil lamp. He went back and forth between the dark and light, bringing pots and dishes and food, and nagging with deep satisfaction, in a mixture of English and Afrikaans. 'You want *koeksusters*, so I make *koeksusters*. You ask me this morning. So I got to make the oil nice and hot, I got to get everything ready ... It's a little bit slow. Yes, I know. But I can't get everything quick, quick. You hurry tonight, you don't want wait, then it's better you have *koeksusters* on Saturday, then I'm got time in the afternoon, I do it nice ... Yes, I think next time it's better ...'

Piet was a good cook. 'I've taught my boy how to make everything', the young man always told people, back in Francistown. 'He can even make *koeksusters*', he had told the girl's mother, in one of those silences of the woman's disapproval that it was so difficult to fill. He had had a hard time, trying to overcome the prejudice of the girl's parents against the sort of life he could offer her. He had managed to convince them that the life was not impossible, and they had given their consent to the marriage, but they still felt that the life was unsuitable, and his desire to please and reassure them had made him anxious to see it with their eyes and so forestall, by changes, their objections. The girl was a farm girl, and would not pine for town life, but, at the same time, he could not deny to her parents that living on a farm with her family around her, and neighbours only thirty or forty miles away, would be very different from living two hundred and twenty miles from a town or village, alone with him in a road camp 'surrounded by a gang of kaffirs all day', as her mother had said. He himself simply did not think at all about what the girl would do while he was out on the road; and as for the girl, until it was over, nothing could exist for her but the wedding, with her two little sisters in pink walking behind her, and her dress that she didn't recognize herself in, being made at the dressmaker's and the cake that was ordered with a tiny china bride and groom in evening dress, on the top.

He looked at the scored table, and the rim of the open jam tin, and the salt cellar with a piece of brown paper tied neatly over the broken top, and said to Piet, 'You must do eveything nice when the missus comes.'

'*Baas*?'

They looked at each other and it was not really necessary to say anything.

'You must make the table properly and do everything clean.'

'Always I make everything clean. Why you say now I must make clean —'

The young man bent his head over his food, dismissing him.

While he ate his mind went automatically over the changes that would have to be made for the girl. He was not used to visualizing situations, but to dealing with what existed. It was like a lesson learned by rote; he knew the totality of what was needed, but if he found himself confronted by one of the component details, he foundered: he did not recognize it or know how to deal with it. The boys must keep out of the way. That was the main thing. Piet would have to come to the caravan quite a lot, to cook and clean. The boys — especially the boys who were responsible for the maintenance of the lorries and road-making equipment — were always coming with questions, what to do about this and that. They'd mess things up, otherwise. He spat out a piece of gristle he could not swallow; his mind went to something else. The women over there — they could do the washing for the girl. They were such a raw bunch of kaffirs, would they ever be able to do anything right? Twenty boys and about five of their women — you couldn't hide them under a thorn bush. They just mustn't hang around, that's all. They must just understand that they mustn't hang around. He looked round keenly through the shadow-puppets of the half-dark on the margin of his fire's light; the voices, companionably quieter, now, intermittent over food, the echoing *chut*! of wood being chopped, the thin film of a baby's wail through which all these sounded — they were on their own side. Yet he felt an odd, rankling suspicion.

His thoughts shuttled, as he ate, in a slow and painstaking way that he had never experienced before in his life — he was worrying. He sucked on a tooth; Piet, Piet, that kaffir talks such a hell of a lot. How's Piet going to stop talking, talking every time he comes near? If he talks to her ... Man, it's sure he'll talk to her. He thought, in actual words, what he would say to Piet about this; the words were like those unsayable things that people write on walls for others to see in private moments, but that are never spoken in their mouths.

Piet brought coffee and *koeksusters* and the young man did not look at him.

But the *koeksusters* were delicious, crisp, sticky, and sweet, and as he felt the familiar substance and taste on his tongue, alternating with the hot bite of the coffee, he at once became occupied with the pure happiness of eating as a child is fully occupied with a bag of sweets. *Koeksusters* never failed to give him this innocent, total pleasure. When first he had taken the job of overseer to the road gang, he had had strange, restless hours at night and on Sundays. It seemed that he was hungry. He ate but never felt satisfied. He walked about all that time, like a hungry creature. One Sunday he actually set out to walk (the Roads Department was very strict about the use of the ten-tonner for private purposes) the fourteen miles across the sand to the cattle-dipping post where the government cattle officer and his wife, Afrikaners like himself and the only other white people between the road camp and Francistown, lived in their corrugated-iron house. By a coincidence, they had decided to drive over and see him, that day, and they had met him a little less than halfway, when he was already slowed and dazed by heat. But shortly after that Piet had taken over the cooking of his meals and the care of his person, and Piet had even learned to make *koeksusters*, according to instructions given to the young man by the cattle officer's wife. The *koeksusters*, a childhood treat that he could indulge in whenever he liked, seemed to mark his settling down; the solitary camp became a personal way of life, with its own special arrangements and indulgences.

'*Ou Piet! Kèrel!* What did you do to the *koeksusters*, hey?' he called out joyously.

A shout came that meant 'Right away'. The black man appeared, drying his hands on a rag, with the diffident, kidding manner of someone who knows he has excelled himself.

'Whatsa matter with the *koeksusters*, man?'

Piet shrugged. 'You must tell me. I don't know what's matter.'

'Here, bring me some more, man.' The young man shoved the empty plate at him, with a grin. And as the other went off, laughing, the young man called. 'You must always make them like that, see?'

He liked to drink at celebrations, at weddings or Christmas, but he wasn't a man who drank his brandy every day. He would have two brandies on a Saturday afternoon, when the week's work was over, and for the rest of the time, the bottle that he brought from Francistown when he went to collect stores lay in the chest in his tent. But on this last night he got up from the fire on impulse and went over to the tent to fetch the bottle (one thing he didn't do, he didn't expect a kaffir to handle his drink for him; it was too much of a temptation to put in their way). He brought a glass with him, too, one of a set of six made of tinted imitation cut glass, and he poured himself a tot and stretched out his legs where he could feel the warmth of the fire through the soles of his boots. The nights were not cold, until the wind came up at two or three in the morning, but there was a clarifying chill to the air; now and then a figure came over from the black men's camp to put another log on the fire whose flames had dropped and become blue. The young man felt inside himself a similar low incandescence; he poured himself another brandy. The long yelping of the jackals prowled the sky without, like the wind about a house; there was no house, but the sounds beyond the light his fire tremblingly inflated into the dark — that jumble of meaningless voices, crying babies, coughs, and hawking — had built walls to enclose and a roof to shelter. He was exposed, turning naked to space on the sphere of the world as the speck that is a fly plastered on the window of an aeroplane, but he was not aware of it.

The lilt of various kinds of small music began and died in the dark; threads of notes, blown and plucked, that disappeared under the voices. Presently a huge man whose thick black body had strained apart every seam in his ragged pants and shirt loped silently into the light and dropped just within it, not too near the fire. His feet, intimately crossed, were cracked and weathered like driftwood. He held to his mouth a one-stringed instrument shaped like a lyre, made out of a half-moon of bent wood with a ribbon of dried palm leaf tied from tip to tip. His big lips rested gently on the strip and while he blew, his one hand, by controlling the vibration of the palm leaf, made of his breath a small, faint, perfect music. It was caught by the very limits of the capacity of the human ear; it was almost out of range. The first music men ever heard, when they began to stand upright among the rushes at the river, might have been like it. When it died away it was difficult to notice at what point it really had gone.

'Play that other one', said the young man, in Tswana. Only the smoke from his pipe moved.

The pink-palmed hands settled down round the instrument. The thick, tender lips were wet once. The faint desolate voice spoke again, so lonely a music that it came to the player and listener as if they heard it inside themselves. This time the player took a short stick in his other hand and, while he blew, scratched it back and forth inside the curve of the lyre, where the notches cut there

42

produced a dry, shaking slithering sound, like the far-off movement of dancers' feet. There were two or three figures with more substance than the shadows, where the firelight merged with the darkness. They came and squatted. One of them had half a paraffin tin, with a wooden neck and other attachments of gut and wire. When the lyre-player paused, lowering his piece of stick and leaf slowly, in ebb, from his mouth, and wiping his lips on the back of his hand, the other began to play. It was a thrumming, repetitive, banjo tune. The young man's boot patted the sand in time to it and he took it up with hand-claps once or twice. A thin, yellowish man in an old hat pushed his way to the front past sarcastic remarks and twittings and sat on his haunches with a little clay bowl between his feet. Over its mouth there was a keyboard of metal tongues. After some exchange, he played it and the others sang low and nasally, bringing a few more strollers to the fire. The music came to an end, pleasantly, and started up again, like a breath drawn. In one of the intervals the young man said, 'Let's have a look at that contraption of yours, isn't it a new one?' and the man to whom he signalled did not understand what was being said to him but handed over his paraffin-tin mandolin with pride and also with amusement at his own handiwork.

The young man turned it over, twanged it once, grinning and shaking his head. Two bits of string and an old jam tin and they'll make a whole band, man. He'd heard them playing some crazy-looking things. The circle of faces watched him with pleasure; they laughed and lazily remarked to each other; it was a funny-looking thing, all right, but it worked. The owner took it back and played it, clowning a little. The audience laughed and joked appreciatively; they were sitting close in to the fire now, painted by it. 'Next week' the young man raised his voice gaily – 'next week when I come back, I bring radio with me, plenty real music. All the big white bands play over it –' Someone who had once worked in Johannesburg said, 'Satchmo', and the others took it up, understanding that this was the word for what the white man was going to bring from town. Satchmo. Satch-mo. They tried it out, politely. 'Music, just like at a big white dance in town. Next week.' A friendly, appreciative silence fell, with them all resting back in the warmth of the fire and looking at him indulgently. A strange thing happened to him. He felt hot, over first his neck, then his ears and his face. It didn't matter, of course; by next week they would have forgotten. They wouldn't expect it. He shut down his mind on a picture of them, hanging round the caravan to listen, and him coming out on the steps to tell them –.

He thought for a moment that he would give them the rest of the

bottle of brandy. Hell, no, man, it was mad. If they got the taste for
the stuff, they'd be pinching it all the time. He'd give Piet some
sugar and yeast and things from the stores, for them to make beer
tomorrow when he was gone. He put his hands deep in his pockets
and stretched out to the fire with his head sunk on his chest. The
lyre-player picked up his flimsy piece of wood again, and slowly
what the young man was feeling inside himself seemed to find a
voice; up into the night beyond the fire, it went, uncoiling from his
breast and bringing ease. As if it had been made audible out of
infinity and could be returned to infinity at any point, the lonely
voice of the lyre went on and on. Nobody spoke, the barriers of
tongues fell with silence. The whole dirty tide of worry and planning
had gone out of the young man. The small, high moon, outshone by
a spiky spread of cold stars, repeated the shape of the lyre. He sat
for he was not aware how long, just as he had for so many other
nights, with the stars at his head and the fire at his feet.

But at last the music stopped and time began again. There was
tonight; there was tomorrow, when he was going to drive to Francistown. He stood up; the company fragmented. The lyre-player blew
his nose into his fingers. Dusty feet took their accustomed weight.
They went off to their tents and he went off to his. Faint plangencies
followed them. The young man gave a loud, ugly, animal yawn, the
sort of unashamed personal noise a man can make when he lives
alone. He walked very slowly across the sand; it was dark but he
knew the way more surely than with his eyes. 'Piet! Hey!' he bawled
as he reached his tent. 'You get up early tomorrow, eh? And I don't
want to hear the lorry won't start. You get it going and then you call
me. D'you hear?'

He was lighting the oil lamp that Piet had left ready on the chest
and as it came up softly it brought the whole interior of the tent with
it: the chest, the bed, the clock, and the coy smiling face of the
seventeen-year-old girl. He sat down on the bed, sliding his palms
through the silky fur of the kaross. He drew a breath and held it for
a moment, looking round purposefully. And then he picked up the
photograph, folded the cardboard support back flat to the frame,
and put it in the chest with all his other things, ready for the
journey.

Notes

kaross — blanket made of animal-hide

Ou Piet, ek wag — Old Piet, I'm waiting

koeksusters — Afrikaans: 'a deep-fried twisted or plaited doughnut immediately
dipped in syrup' (Branford Dictionary)

kêrel — Afrikaans: 'chap' or 'man'

Rain is crucial to the people of Africa. Have a look at two different atmospheres concerning rain in these two poems:

Adriaanspoort

Sipho Sepamla

Down there below
where I can see no spoor
of man or animal
there is a winding
of what used to be
there is a swaying
of lanky tufts of grass
there is a meandering
of leafy protea trees
there is an ageing
of variegated pelindaba rocks
and there is a thought
of dead spirits
once clashing by day
only to retreat at sunset
leaving these parts wild at night
yet serene under the moon

where I stand
there is no stench with which to live
only the giddy smell of braaied boerewors
already the plastic plates are full of stywe mielie-pap
a table is laden with sliced cheese and green salads
for amidst the chattering of adults in French
and the fooling around of our children in no language of words

we are going to revel
beyond the mischievous hand of man

there is a spirit moving where we are
we turn faces to avoid it
hardly being successful
for we are part of the being of things

there are clouds gathering above our heads
we say it will not rain
hardly being correct
for the earth needs to be swept at times

it rains! ... pula! ... it rains! ... pula!

Notes

poort — Afrikaans: a narrow pass or river-ford

spoor — Afrikaans: animal track

pelindaba — Pelindaba is an area near the Hartebeespoort Dam in the Pretoria
district

braai — Afrikaans: a barbecue, also 'braaivleis'

boerewors — Afrikaans: sausage

stywe — Afrikaans: stiff

mielie-pap — Afrikaans: a porridge of mealie-meal, often eaten with meat

Cattle in the Rain

Musaemura Zimunya

Nothing has no end,
it is true.
This rain used to soak us in the pastures
and the cattle would not stop to graze,
they would not be driven to the kraal,
it made me cry and curse sometimes
and I used to wish I was born for the skirt.
Just imagine penetrating the wet bush
almost doubled up
with a heavy smelling coned up jute sack
as a rain coat,
pebbles of water pounding on the head,
very irritating, too.
Sometimes an angry wasp disturbed by the foregoing cows
stabbed you on the cursing lips
and in the frantic stampede,
wet thorns snapped at random in your benumbed feet.
And the rain does not cease
and the cows just go on.

Come to the kraal –
This ox, called Gatooma,
stands still before the rest,
his ghost of silent disapproval shattering to your mind,
listening, listening to nothing at all,
and I knew then that I had to call for help.
But people at home in warm huts
could hardly hear me through the maddening rain.
This ox, tail high,
at two sniffs and a cajole,
all meant to humiliate
would crash through the thin bush
leaving me running weakly
sobbing at each step
a bone of anger blocking my breath,
chugging after the rhythmic hooves hammering the earth.
and still it rained
and the cows went skelter
and the rain swept the salty tears
and watery mucus into my lips.

Notes

kraal – used in this sense, 'an enclosure or pen for farm-animals' (Branford Dictionary)

coned up jute sack – you take a hessian sack by its two corners, and fold one corner inside, into the other. This makes a cone-shape to fit over your head, pretty effective as a raincoat. Men who carry sacks of coal often protect their heads and shoulders by wearing such a cone-sack.

Sweet-water

Guy Butler

While packing gold butter, lace doilies, buck biltong,
spring chickens, frilled aprons, cut flowers, dried peaches
into the boot and back seat of the car,
Aunt Betsy, convener of twenty committees
and big queen bee of the church bazaar
barked gently at the garden 'boy':
'Boesak! Where's master? Find him! Tell him
that we are waiting.' Then, smiling, to me:
'Just like your Uncle, selfish old dreamer.'

When Uncle Danby took the wheel,
his hands would hover, seize it, feel
it for tension like one who tries
the reins of a horse who sometimes shies;
his legs, once expert with stirrups and spurs,
had never quite mastered these brakes and gears.
As the clutch was released the back wheels sprayed
the hens with a shrapnel of gravel; dismayed
they took to the trees, while parcels galore
rocketted onto the Buick's floor.
No word of comment from the old folk:
was this start normal? Or beyond a joke?

In silence we sailed with white winter grasses
swishing the mudguards; silence, enlarged
by the drone of the engine, by a startled korhaan
rising, clattering, into the sky: silence
seeping from petrified seas in the sandstone, so huge
that when I opened a gate the squeak of its socket
sounded small and sharp as a cricket
where grumbling breakers smother the old Cape granite
at dusk when a long Southwester falls.

'So you're going to 'Vahsity?
That's what they called it,
them Pommie Awficers
in the Bah Wah.'

He chuckled, remembering
accents and mannerisms
of elegant red-necked subalterns
whose blue-blood pedigrees
went back to the Battle of Hastings
rather than Eighteen Twenty.

'Vahsity!'

'Yes, Uncle.'

'Man, I only made standard four.
Dad called us back to the farm.
He had his reasons —
a run of bad seasons

locust swarms in the sky
dark as the day of doom —
Oh long, Oh long before
the ostrich feather boom.

At the word 'feather' Aunt Betsy's hand
unconsciously fluttered towards her antique hat.
Ironstone koppies like dead volcanic islands
rising purple and black from oceans of grass,
fawn-soft grass lapping the parallel shales
of mountains thrusting daring capes and headlands
from continents still hidden over either horizon.

And here and there, as light as a drift of flotsam,
a store, an avenue, a kraal or a farm;
or a new-shorn flock of merinos like a trail of spume.

Not far ahead the Kwaai River
trailed its tawdry fringe of mimosas across the flats.
Soon our red-road-ribbon
would cross the stream, on the brand-new causeway,
the pride of the district:
opened last month by our MPC.
with a speets on nashonil prowgriss
followed by braaivleis and brandy —
O concertinas and moonlight
and singing of Sarie Marais.

'Along this road,
come rain, come shine,
my brothers and me
we drove stock to the fair.
What I remember best
was dust.
Man, I must
of swallowed a muid or two
of good Karoo soil in my time.
But there was also
the sweetest water.'

He ran his tongue round his bearded lips

Approaching the river we saw the causeway,
concrete, white, with neat crenellations
like a Beau Geste fort fronting the river,
but wide enough for one-way traffic only.
Carefully he eased the car down the slope,
then, slap in the middle, switched off the engine.

Aunt Betsy sat up with a start: 'What? —'

'Man, when I was a boy,' he said.

'Danby!' she cried, 'We're half an hour late!'

His blue eyes quelled her.
'When I was a boy,' he said,
'we always outspanned for the night,
here, among these trees.
There's no sweeter water
in all the district.'

The way he said it, with a smooth small gesture
of the arm from the elbow with the palm flat, downwards,
sent the mind's eye feeling over
the whole Fish River catchment
down South from Dassiedeur and Daggaboer
in great arc North to Teviot
and West-by-North to Spitskopvlei.

'But Danby dear, we're half an hour late!'
I don't think he heard her. Sometimes a greybeard
leaning, listening down the deep well of his years
turns stone-deaf to the fractional present.
Seventy winters through his bones
since first he stopped at Kwaai River.

At the end of the new-fangled causeway
he clambered over the ironstone boulders
and strolled up the river bed to a bend
where seventy centuries had scooped a bowl
in the crazily-cracked substratum of gravel.

Fringed with a palest sand, a large pool in the blue gravel
with a fine and feathery dust upon it

and water boatman tracing
lazy arcs and circles in the sun;
their legs, no longer than an eyelash,
were shaking the reflected sky and making
the far-off images of mountains quake.

I heard a crescendo of hooting
and pictured the chaos at the causeway.
But he was oblivious, busy with things that mattered.

On the sand near the water's edge
he spread his handkerchief, and knelt.
I could hear his old joints creak.
Embarrassed, I knelt nearby.
'Now,' he said, 'you must first
blow the dust from the surface, like this.'

The floating film gave way like wax off apple skin.
The frantic water beetles scattered so quickly
they left the eye blinking at ripples and ripples only.

'Now scoop the water with your hand, but never,
no matter how thirsty you are.
swallow the first.
That's to rinse the dust from your mouth.'

He did so, spitting the water behind him.

'Now,' he said, 'now,
Oh taste how sweet it is.'

Delicately, three times,
the huge and trembling hand
cupped the sweet waters of the Angry River
to his lips, to sip it with a little noise
softer than the whirr of starling wings
from their nest-holes in the bank above us.

When we got to the causeway a dozen cars,
some hooting, were waiting; and old Aunt Betsy
sunk in shame and sulks. Unabashed
he lifted stiff legs onto the pedals
and said, with an ice-breaking twinkle:
'But don't you want to rinse your mouth, my dear?'

Laughter and fury broke together from her:
'When I was a boy, indeed! When
were you ever anything else?'

Turning, he grinned at me. The blue eye said:
'Oh, she don't understand us boys.'

He's dead now, and I am left,
bereft, wondering
to what stream I could take whom
and kneel like that and say:
Taste how sweet it is.

Notes
korhaan — bustard
koppie — Afrikaans: small hill
MPC — Member of the Provincial Council
speets . . . nashonil prowgriss — the poet is having some fun with the South
   African English accent
muid — Afrikaans: a Dutch measure, weighing about 90 kg

The Wind and a Boy

Bessie Head

Like all the village boys, Friedman had a long wind blowing for him,
but perhaps the enchanted wind that blew for him, filled the whole
world with magic.

Until they became ordinary, dull grown men, who drank beer and
made babies, the little village boys were a special set all on their
own. They were kings whom no one ruled. They wandered where
they willed from dawn to dusk and only condescended to come
home at dusk because they were afraid of the horrible things in the

52

dark that might pounce on them. Unlike the little girls who adored household chores and drawing water, it was only now and then that the boys showed themselves as useful attachments to any household. When the first hard rains of summer fell, small dark shapes, quite naked except for their loin-cloths, sped out of the village into the bush. They knew that the first downpour had drowned all the wild rabbits, moles, and porcupines in their burrows in the earth. As they crouched down near the entrances to the burrows, they would see a small drowned nose of an animal peeping out; they knew it had struggled to emerge from its burrow, flooded by the sudden rush of storm water and as they pulled out the animal, they would say, pityingly:

'Birds have more sense than rabbits, moles and porcupines. They build their homes in trees.' but it was hunting made easy, for no matter how hard a boy and his dog ran, a wild rabbit ran ten times faster; a porcupine hurled his poisonous quills into the body; and a mole stayed where he thought it was safe — deep under the ground. So it was with inordinate pride that the boys carried home armfuls of dead animals for their families to feast on for many days. Apart from that, the boys lived very much as they pleased, with the wind and their own games.

Now and then, the activities of a single family could captivate the imagination and hearts of all the people of their surroundings; for years and years, the combination of the boy, Friedman and his grandmother, Sejosenye, made the people of Ga-Sefete-Molemo ward, smile, laugh, then cry.

They smiled at his first two phases. Friedman came home as a small bundle from the hospital, a bundle his grandmother nursed carefully near her bosom and crooned to day and night with extravagant care and tenderness.

'She is like that,' people remarked, 'because he may be the last child she will ever nurse. Sejosenye is old now and will die one of these days, the child is a gift to keep her heart warm.'

Indeed, all Sejosenye's children were grown, married, and had left home. Of all her children, only her last-born daughter was unmarried and Friedman was the result of some casual mating she had indulged in, in a town a hundred miles away where she had a job as a typist. She wanted to return to her job almost immediately, so she handed the child over to her mother and that was that; she could afford to forget him as he had a real mother now. During all the time that Sejosenye haunted the hospital, awaiting her bundle, a friendly foreign doctor named Friedman took a fancy to her maternal, grandmotherly ways. He made a habit of walking out of his path to talk to her. She never forgot it and on receiving her bundle she called the baby, Friedman.

They smiled at his second phase, a small dark shadow who toddled silently and gravely beside a very tall grandmother; wherever the grandmother went, there went Friedman. Most women found this phase of the restless, troublesome toddler tedious; they dumped the toddler onto one of their younger girls and were off to weddings and visits on their own.

'Why can't you leave your handbag at home some times, granny?' they said.

'Oh, he's no trouble,' Sejosenye would reply.

They began to laugh at his third phase. Almost overnight he turned into a tall, spindly-legged, graceful gazelle with large, grave eyes. There was an odd, musical lilt to his speech and when he teased, or was up to mischief, he moved his head on his long thin neck from side to side like a cobra. It was he who became the king of kings of all the boys in his area; he could turn his hand to anything and made the best wire cars with their wheels of shoe polish tins. All his movements were neat, compact, decisive, and for his age he was a boy who knew his own mind. They laughed at his knowingness and certainty on all things, for he was like the grandmother who had had a flaming youth all her own too. Sejosenye had scandalized the whole village in her days of good morals by leaving her own village ward to live with a married man in Ga-Sefete-Molemo ward. She had won him from his wife and married him and then lived down the scandal in the way only natural queens can. Even in old age, she was still impressive. She sailed through the village, head in the air, with a quiet, almost expressionless face. She had developed large buttocks as time went by and they announced their presence firmly in rhythm with her walk.

Another of Sejosenye's certainties was that she was a woman who could plough, but it was like a special gift. Each season, in drought or hail or sun, she removed herself to her lands. She not only ploughed but nursed and brooded over her crops. She was there all the time till the corn ripened and the birds had to be chased off the land, till harvesting and threshing were done; so that even in drought years with their scanty rain, she came home with some crops. She was the envy of all the women of the surroundings.

'Sejosenye always eats fine things in her house,' they said. 'She ploughs and then sits down for many months and enjoys the fruits of her labour.'

The women also envied her beautiful grandson. There was something special there, so that even when Friedman moved into his bad phase, they forgave him crimes other boys received a sound thrashing for. The small boys were terrible thieves who harassed people by stealing their food and money. It was all a part of the games they played but one which people did not like. Of them all, Friedman was the worst thief, so that his name was mentioned more and more in any thieving that had been uncovered.

'But Friedman showed us how to open the window with a knife and string,' the sobbing, lashed boys would protest.

'Friedman isn't as bad as you,' the parents would reply, irrationally. They were hypnotised by a beautiful creature. The boy Friedman, who had become a real nuisance by then, also walked around as though he were special. He couldn't possibly be a thief and he added an aloof, offended, disdainful expression to his pretty face. He wasn't just an ordinary sort of boy in Ga-Sefete-Molemo ward. He was ...

It happened, quite accidentally, that his grandmother told him all those stories about the hunters, warriors, and emissaries of old. She was normally a quiet, absent-minded woman, given to dreaming by herself but she liked to sing the boy a little song now and then as they sat by the outdoor fire. A lot of them were church songs and rather sad; they more or less passed as her bed-time prayer at night – she was one of the old church-goers. Now and then she added a quaint little song to her repertoire and as the nighttime, fire-light flames flickered between them, she never failed to note that this particular song was always well received by the boy. A little light would awaken in his eyes and he would bend forward and listen attentively.

'Welcome, Robinson Crusoe, welcome,' she would sing, in clear, sweet tones. 'How could you stay, so long away, Robinson how could you do so?'

When she was very young, Sejosenye had attended the mission school of the village for about a year: made a slight acquaintance with the ABC and one, two, three, four, five, and the little song about Robinson Crusoe. But girls didn't need an education in those days when ploughing and marriage made up their whole world. Yet Robinson Crusoe lived on as a gay and out-of-context memory of her school-days. One evening the boy leaned forward and asked:

'Is that a special praise-poem song for Robinson Crusoe, grand-mother?'

'Oh yes,' she replied, smiling.

'It appears that the people liked Robinson Crusoe, much,' the boy observed. 'Did he do great things for them?'

'Oh yes,' she said, smiling.

'What great things did he do? the boy asked, pointedly.

'They say he was a hunter who went by Gweta side and killed an elephant all by himself,' she said, making up a story on the spot. 'Oh! In those days, no man could kill an elephant by himself. All the regiments had to join together and each man had to thrust his sword into the side of the elephant before it died. Well, Robinson Crusoe was gone many days and people wondered about him: "Perhaps he has been eaten by a lion," they said. "Robinson likes to be a solitary person and do foolish things. We won't ever go out into the bush by ourselves because we know it is dangerous." Well, one day, Robinson suddenly appeared in their midst and people could see that he had a great thing on his mind. They all gathered around him. He said: "I have killed an elephant for all the people." The people were surprised: "Robinson!" they said. "It is impossible! How did you do it? The very thought of an elephant approaching the village makes us shiver!" And Robinson said: "Ah, people, I saw a terrible sight! I was standing at the feet of the elephant. I was just a small ant. I could not see the world any more. Elephant was above me until his very head touched the sky and his ears spread out like great wings. He was angry but I only looked into one eye which was turning round and round in anger. What to do now? I thought it better to put that eye out. I raised my spear and threw it at the angry eye. People! It went right inside. Elephant said not a word and he fell to one side. Come I will show you what I have done." Then the women cried in joy: "Loo-loo-loo!" They ran to fetch their containers as some wanted the meat of the elephant; some wanted the fat. The men made their knives sharp. They would make shoes and many things from the skin and bones. There was something for all the people in the great work Robinson Crusoe did.'

All this while, as he listened to the story, the boy's eyes had glowed softly. At the end of it, he drew in a long breath.

'Grandmother,' he whispered, adroitly stepping into the role of Robinson Crusoe, the great hunter. 'One day, I'm going to be like that. I'm going to be a hunter like Robinson Crusoe and bring meat to all the people.' He paused for breath and then added tensely: 'And what other great thing did Robinson Crusoe do?'

'Tsaa!' she said, clicking her tongue in exhaustion. 'Am I then going away that I must tell *all* the stories at once?'

Although his image of Robinson Crusoe, the great hunter, was never to grow beyond his everyday boyish activities of pushing wire cars, hunting in the fields for wild rabbits, climbing trees to pull down old bird's nests and yelling out in alarm to find that a small snake now occupied the abandoned abode, or racing against the wind with the spoils of his latest theft, the stories awakened a great tenderness in him. If Robinson Crusoe was not churning up the dust in deadly hand-to-hand combat with an enemy, he was crossing swollen rivers and wild jungles as the great messenger and ambassador of the chief — all his activities were touchingly in aid of or in defence of, the people. One day Friedman expressed this awakened compassion for life in a strange way. After a particularly violent storm, people found their huts invaded by many small mice and they were hard-pressed to rid themselves of these pests. Sejosenye ordered Friedman to kill the mice.

'But grandmother,' he protested. 'They have come to us for shelter. They lost all their homes in the storm. It's better that I put them in a box and carry them out into the fields again once the rains are over.'

She had laughed in surprise at this and spread the story around among her women friends, who smiled tenderly then said to their own offspring: 'Friedman isn't as bad as you.'

Life and its responsibilities began to weigh down heavily on Friedman as he approached his fourteenth year. Less time was spent in boyish activities. He grew more and more devoted to his grandmother and concerned to assist her in every way. He wanted a bicycle so that he might run up and down to the shops for her, deliver messages, or do any other chore she might have in mind. His mother, who worked in a town far away, sent him the money to purchase the bicycle. The gift brought the story of his life abruptly to a close.

Towards the beginning of the rainy season, he accompanied his grandmother to her lands which were some twenty miles outside the village. They sowed seed together after the hired tractor had turned up the land but the boy's main chore was to keep the household pot filled with meat. Sometimes they ate birds Friedman had trapped, sometimes they ate fried tortoise-meat or wild rabbit; there was always something as the bush abounded with animal life. Sejosenye only had to take a bag of mealie meal, packets of sugar, tea, and powdered milk as provisions for their stay at the lands; meat was never a problem. Mid-way through the ploughing season, she began to run out of sugar, tea, and milk.

'Friedman,' she said that evening. 'I shall wake you early tomorrow morning. You will have to take the bicycle into the village and purchase some more sugar, tea, and milk.'

He was up at dawn with the birds, a solitary figure cycling on a pathway through the empty bush. By nine, he had reached the village and first made his way to Ga-Sefete-Molemo ward and the yard of a friend of his grandmother, who gave him a cup of tea and a plate of porridge. Then he put one foot on the bicycle and turned to smile at the woman with his beautiful gazelle eyes. His smile was to linger vividly before her for many days as a short while later, hard pounding feet came running into her yard to report that Friedman was dead.

He pushed the bicycle through the winding, sandy pathway of the village ward, reached the high embankment of the main road, peddled vigorously up it and out of the corner of his eye, saw a small green truck speeding towards him. In the devil-may-care fashion of all the small boys, he cycled right into its path, turned his head and smiled appealingly at the driver. The truck caught him on the front bumper, squashed the bicycle and dragged the boy along at a crazy speed for another hundred yards, dropped him and careered on another twenty yards before coming to a halt. The boy's pretty face was a smear all along the road and he only had a torso left.

People of Ga-Sefete-Molemo ward never forgot the last coherent words Sejosenye spoke to the police. A number of them climbed into the police truck and accompanied it to her lands. They saw her walk slowly and enquiringly towards the truck, they heard the matter-of-fact voice of the policeman announce the death, then they heard Sejosenye say piteously: 'Can't you return those words back?'

She turned away from them, either to collect her wits or the few possessions she had brought with her. Her feet and buttocks quivered anxiously as she stumbled towards her hut. Then her feet tripped her up and she fell to the ground like a stunned log.

The people of Ga-Sefete-Molemo ward buried the boy Friedman but none of them would go near the hospital where Sejosenye lay. The stories brought to them by way of the nurses were too terrible for words. They said the old woman sang and laughed and talked to herself all the time. So they merely asked each other: 'Have you been to see Mma-Sejosenye?' 'I'm afraid I cannot. It would kill my heart.' Two weeks later, they buried her.

As was village habit, the incident was discussed thoroughly from all sides till it was understood. In this timeless, sleepy village, the goats stood and suckled their young ones on the main road or lay down and took their afternoon naps there. The motorists either stopped for them or gave way. But it appeared that the driver of the truck had neither brakes on his car nor a driving license. He belonged to the new, rich civil-servant class whose salaries had become fantastically high since independence. They had to have cars in keeping with their new status; they had to have any car, as long as it was a car; they were in such a hurry about everything that they couldn't be bothered to take driving lessons. And thus progress, development, and a pre-occupation with status and living-standards first announced themselves to the village. It looked like being an ugly story with many decapitated bodies on the main road.

Notes

ward — in the sense Bessie Head is using it, a ward is a section, an area, of a village in Botswana

Compare these two incisive and acutely observed views of two small railway stations, both coincidentally in Natal province:

Cookhouse Station

Chris Zithulele Mann

(*for Jackie*)

If you ever pass through Cookhouse Station
make certain you see what is there,
not just the long neat platform beneath the escarpment,
and the red buckets
and the red-and-white booms,
but the beetle as well
which sings like a tireless lover
high in the gum-tree all the hot day.

And whether your stay is short,
and whether your companions
beg you to turn from the compartment window
does not matter, only make certain you see
the rags of the beggarman's coat
before you choose to sit again.

And though there might be no passengers
waiting in little heaps of luggage
when you look, make certain you see
the migrant workers with their blankets
as well as the smiling policeman,
the veiled widow as well as the girl

the trainee-soldiers whistle at, otherwise
you have not passed that way at all.

And if it is a midday in December
with a light so fierce
all the shapes of things quiver
and mingle, make certain you see
the shades of those who once lived there,
squatting in the cool of the blue-gum tree,
at ease in the fellowship of the afterdeath.

And if you ever pass through Cookhouse Station
make certain you greet these men well, otherwise
you have not passed that way at all.

Amagoduka at Glencoe Station

Mbuyiseni Oswald Mtshali

We travelled a long journey
through the wattle forests of Vryheid,
crossed the low-levelled Blood River
whose water flowed languidly
as if dispirited for the
shattered glory of my ancestors.

We passed the coalfields of Dundee —
blackheads in the wrinkled face
of Northern Zululand —
until our train ultimately came
to a hissing stop at Glencoe.

Many people got off
leaving the enraged train
to snort and charge at the night
on its way to Durban.

The time was 8 p.m.
I picked up my suitcase,
sagging under the weight of a heavy overcoat
I shambled to the 'non-European Males' waiting room.

The room was crowded
the air hung, a pall of choking odour,
rotten meat, tobacco and sour beer.

Windows were shut tight
against the sharp bite of winter.

Amagoduka sat on bare floor
their faces sucking the warmth
of the coal fire crackling in the corner.

They chewed dried bread
scooped corned beef with rusty knives,
and drank *mqombothi* from the plastic can
which they passed from mouth to mouth.

They spoke animatedly
and laughed in thunderous peals.

A girl peeped through the door,
they shuddered at the sudden cold blast,
jumped up to fondle and leer at her

Hau! ngena Sis — Oh! come in sister!'

She shied like a frightened filly
banged the door and bolted.

They broke into a tumultuous laughter.

One of them picked up a guitar
plucked it with broken fingernails
caressed its strings with a castor oil bottle —

it sighed like a jilted girl,
'You play down! Phansi! Play D' he whispered.

Another joined in with a concertina,
its sound fluttered in flowery notes
like a butterfly picking pollen from flower to flower.

The two began to sing,
their voices crying for the mountains

and the hills of Msinga, stripped naked of
their green garment.

They crossed rivers and streams,
gouged dry by the sun rays,
where lowing cattle genuflected
for a blade of grass and a drop of water
on riverbeds littered with carcasses and bones.

They spoke of hollow-cheeked maidens
heaving drums of brackish water
from a far away fountain.

They told of big-bellied babies
sucking festering fingers
instead of their mothers' shrivelled breasts.

Two cockroaches
as big as my overcoat buttons
jived across the floor
snatched meat and bread crumbs
and scurried back to their hideout.

The whole group joined in unison:
various eyes peered through frosted windows
'*Ekhaya bafowethu*! — Home brothers!'

Notes
amagoduka — Zulu: 'migrant labourers: 'returning ones' who go home at regular
    intervals' (Branford Dictionary); plural of 'goduka' (see note on Matshoba, *Call
    Me Not a Man*)
mqombothi — traditionally brewed beer
Phansi! — Down!

Points for discussion
● In THE BRIDEGROOM how do you imagine everyone — young man,
Piet, new wife, work gang — will react and adjust to the arrival of the
new person in their small community? The word *community* seems oddly
appropriate: what in the story suggests it?
● How would you described the mood of ADRIAANSPOORT? Do you
notice how the poet has selected particular elements of his surroundings
to create this mood?

62

• How different a mood is created in CATTLE IN THE RAIN! Again, it is a matter of selecting specific items carefully, ones that will evoke the feeling you wish to convey. Do you recollect chores you had to do as a small child that left you shedding tears of frustration?

• A long poem, SWEET-WATER — and one that raises the question of what a poem is. Could the poem just as easily have been written as prose? Some of it certainly lends itself to re-formatting, eg look at stanza 5 on page 50 printed as prose: 'At the end of the new-fangled causeway he clambered over the ironstone boulders and strolled up the river bed to a bend where seventy centuries had scooped a bowl in the crazily-cracked substratum of gravel.' So, what is the difference? Some like to say that poetry gives a new insight into an experience; and that, by shaping and refining it in words, sounds and rhythms, the writer gives the experience a particular significance. Is that true of this poem?

• Two points about the story by Bessie Head, THE WIND AND A BOY: First, what do you think about the way she cuts out the element of suspense by telling you a page and a half before the end that the boy is going to die? Does that in any way weaken the story, or do you find it good in that she is not artificially 'manufacturing' an ending? Second, does the way she has written the story prepare you at all for the last paragraph? Is the story a good fictional illustration of the sociological point she makes here — or does the sociological point sound 'tagged on' to you?

• Make a list of the different items Mann and Mtshali have decided to note and observe in their two 'station' poems. Can you detect a difference in the authors' viewpoints? Is it possible — or sensible — to say which is the better poem?

In the city

In recent years much of the focus of Southern African writing has moved from the 'veld and vlei' adventures of the country to the very different experiences of the city. You can pinpoint some of the major urban centres in these pieces: Cape Town (la Guma, Rive, Dangor), Durban (Pillay, Livingstone), Johannesburg (Manaka) and the various black and 'Coloured' townships around it (Mtshali, Johennesse). The Xolile Guma story is set in Mbabane in Swaziland, and the two Mungoshi poems in Zimbabwe:

from A Walk in the Night

Alex la Guma

ONE

The young man dropped from the trackless tram just before it stopped at Castle Bridge. He dropped off, ignoring the stream of late-afternoon traffic rolling in from the suburbs, bobbed and ducked the cars and buses, the big, rumbling delivery trucks, deaf to the shouts and curses of the drivers, and reached the pavement.

Standing there, near the green railings around the public convenience, he lighted a cigarette, jostled by the lines of workers going home, the first trickle of a stream that would soon be flowing towards Hanover Street. He looked right through them, refusing to see them, nursing a little growth of anger the way one caresses the beginnings of a toothache with the tip of the tongue.

Around him the buzz and hum of voices and the growl of traffic blended into one solid mutter of sound which he only half-heard, his thoughts concentrated upon the pustule of rage and humiliation that was continuing to ripen deep down within him.

The young man wore jeans that had been washed several times and which were now left with a pale-blue colour flecked with old grease stains and the newer, darker ones of that day's work in the sheet metal factory, and going white along the hard seams. The jeans had brass buttons, and the legs were too long, so that they had to be turned up six inches at the bottom. He also wore an old khaki shirt and over it a rubbed and scuffed and worn leather coat with slanting pockets and woolen wrists. His shoes were of the moccasin type, with leather thongs stitching the saddle to the rest of the uppers. They had been a bright tan once, but now they were worn a dark brown, beginning to crack in the grooves across the insteps. The thongs had broken in two places on one shoe and in one place on the other.

He was a well-built young man of medium height, and he had dark curly hair, slightly brittle but not quite kinky, and a complexion the colour of worn leather. If you looked closely you could see the dark shadow caused by premature shaving along his cheeks and around the chin and upper lip. His eyes were very dark brown, the whites not quite clear, and he had a slightly protuberant upper lip. His hands were muscular, with ridges of vein, the nails broad and thick like little shells, and rimmed with black from handling machine oil and grease. The backs of his hands, like his face, were brown, but the palms were pink with tiny ridges of yellow-white callouses. Now his dark brown eyes had hardened a little with sullenness.

He half-finished the cigarette, and threw the butt into the garden behind the fence around the public convenience. The garden of the convenience was laid out in small terraces and rockeries, carefully cultivated by the City Council, with many different kinds of rock plants, flowers, cacti and ornamental trees. This the young man did not see, either, as he stepped off the pavement, dodging the traffic again and crossing the intersection to the Portuguese restaurant opposite.

In front of the restaurant the usual loungers hung around under the overhanging verandah, idling, talking, smoking, waiting. The window was full of painted and printed posters advertising dances, concerts, boxing-matches, meetings, and some of the loungers stood looking at them, commenting on the ability of the fighters or the popularity of the dance bands. The young man, his name was Michael Adonis, pushed past them and went into the cafe.

It was warm inside, with the smell of frying oil and fat and tobacco smoke. People sat in the booths or along a wooden table down the centre of the place, eating or engaged in conversation. Ancient strips of flypaper hung from the ceiling dotted with their victims and the floor was stained with spilled coffee, grease and crushed cigarette butts; the walls marked with the countless rubbing of soiled shoulders and grimy hands. There was a general atmosphere of shabbiness about the cafe, but not unmixed with a sort of home-liness for the unending flow of derelicts, bums, domestic workers off duty, in-town-from-the-country folk who had no place to eat except there, and working people who stopped by on their way home. There were taxi-drivers too, and the rest of the mould that accumulated on the fringes of the underworld beyond Castle Bridge: loiterers, prostitutes, *fab-fee* numbers runners, petty gangsters, drab and frayed-looking thugs.

Michael Adonis looked around the cafe and saw Willieboy sitting at the long table that ran down the middle of the room. Willieboy was young and dark and wore his kinky hair brushed into a point above his forehead. He wore a sportscoat over a yellow T-shirt and a crucifix around his neck, more as a flamboyant decoration than as an act of religious devotion. He had yellowish eyeballs and big white teeth and an air of nonchalance, like the outward visible sign of his distorted pride in the terms he had served in a reformatory and once in prison for assault.

He grinned, showing his big teeth as Michael Adonis strolled up, and said, 'Hoit, pally,' in greeting. He had finished a meal of steak and chips and was lighting a cigarette.

'Howzit,' Michael Adonis said surlily, sitting down opposite him. They were not very close friends, but had been thrown together in the whirlpool world of poverty, petty crime and violence of which that cafe was an outpost.

'Nice, boy, nice. You know me, mos. Always take it easy. How goes it with you?'

'Strolling again. Got pushed out of my job at the facktry.'

'How come then?'

'Answered back to a effing white rooker. Foreman.'

'Those whites. What happened?'

'That white bastard was lucky I didn't pull him up good. He had been asking for it a long time. Everytime a man goes to the piss-house he starts moaning. Jesus Christ, the way he went on you'd think a man had to wet his pants rather than take a minute off. Well, he picked on me for going for a leak and I told him to go to hell.'

'Ja,' Willieboy said. 'Working for whites. Happens all the time, man. Me, I never work for no white john. Not even brown one. To hell with work. Work, work, work, where does it get you? Not me, pally.'

The Swahili waiter came over, dark and shiny with perspiration, his white apron grimy and spotted with egg-yolk. Michael Adonis said: 'Steak and chips, and bring the tomato sauce, too.' To Willieboy he said: 'Well, a juba's got to live. Called me a cheeky black bastard. Me, I'm not black. Anyway I said he was a no-good pore-white and he calls the manager and they gave me my pay and tell me to muck off out of it. White sonofabitch. I'll get him.'

'No, man, me I don't work. Never worked a bogger yet. Whether you work or don't, you live anyway, somehow. I haven't starved to death, have I? Work. Eff work.'

'I'll get him,' Michael Adonis said. His food came, handed to him on a chipped plate with big slices of bread on the side. He began to eat, chewing sullenly. Willieboy got up and strolled over to the juke-box, slipped a sixpenny piece into the slot. Michael Adonis ate silently, his anger mixing with a resentment for a fellow who was able to take life so easy.

Music boomed out of the speaker, drowning the buzz of voices in the cafe, and Willieboy stood by the machine, watching the disc spinning behind the lighted glass.

> When mah baby lef' me,
> She gimme a mule to rahd . . .
> When mah baby lef' me,
> She gimme a mule to rahd . . .

Michael Adonis went on eating, thinking over and over again, That sonavabitch, that bloody white sonavabitch, I'll get him. Anger seemed to make him ravenous and he bolted his food. While he was drinking his coffee from the thick, cracked cup three men came into the cafe, looked around the place, and then came over to him.

One of the men wore a striped, navy-blue suit and a highcrowned brown hat. He had a brown, bony face with knobby cheekbones, hollow cheeks and a bony, ridged jawline, all giving him a scrofulous look. The other two with him were youths and they wore new, lightweight tropical suits with pegged trousers and gaudy neckties. They had young, yellowish, depraved faces and thick hair shiny with brilliantine. One of them had a ring with a skull-and-crossbones on one finger. The eyes in the skull were cheap red stones, and he toyed with the ring all the time as if he wished to draw attention to it.

They pulled out chairs and sat down, and the man in the striped suit said: 'Het, Mikey.'

'Hullo.'

'They fired me.'

'Hell, just near the big days, too.' The man spoke as if there was something wrong with his throat; in a high, cracked voice, like the twang of a flat guitar string.

The boy with the ring said, 'We're looking for Sockies. You seen him?'

The man in the striped suit, who was called Foxy, said, 'We got a job on tonight. We want him for look-out man.'

'You don't have to tell him,' the boy with the ring said, looking at Foxy. He had a thin, olive-skinned face with down on his upper lip, and the whites of his eyes were unnaturally yellow.

'He's okay,' Foxy told him. 'Mikey's a pal of ours. Don't I say, Mikey?'

'I don't give over what you boys do,' Michael Adonis replied. He took a packet of cigarettes from the pocket of his leather coat and offered it around. They each took one.

When the cigarettes were lighted the one who had not spoken yet, said: 'Why don't we ask him to come in? We can do without Sockies if you say he's okay.' He had an old knife scar across his right cheekbone and looked very young and brutal.

Michael Adonis said nothing.

'Mikey's a good boy,' Foxy said, grinning with the cigarette in his mouth. 'He ain't like you blerry gangsters.'

'Well,' said the scarfaced boy. 'If you see Sockies, tell him we looking for him.'

'Where'll he get you?' Michael Adonis asked.

'He knows where to find us,' Foxy said.

'Come on then, man,' the boy with the scarface said. 'Let's stroll.'

'Okay, Mikey,' Foxy said as they got up.

'Okay.'

'Okay, pally,' the scarfaced boy said.

They went out of the cafe and Michael Adonis watched them go. He told himself they were a hardcase lot. The anger over having got the sack from his job had left him then, and he was feeling a little better. He picked up the bill from the table and went over to the counter to pay it.

Outside the first workers were streaming past towards Hanover, on their way to their homes in the quarter known as District Six. The trackless trams were full, rocking their way up the rise at Castle Bridge, the overflow hanging onto the grips of the platform. Michael Adonis watched the crowds streaming by, smoking idly, his mind wandering towards the stockinged legs of the girls, the chatter and hum of traffic brushing casually across his hearing. Up ahead a neon sign had already come on, pale against the late sunlight, flicking on and off, on and off, on and off.

He left the entrance of the cafe and fell into the stream, walking up towards the District, past the shopfronts with the adverts of shoes, underwear, Coca-Cola, cigarettes.

Inside the cafe the juke-box had stopped playing and Willieboy turned away from it, looking for Michael Adonis, and found that he had left.

TWO

Up ahead the music shops were still going full blast, the blare of records all mixed up so you could not tell one tune from another. Shopkeepers, Jewish, Indian, and Greek, stood in the doorways along the arcade of stores on each side of the street, waiting to welcome last-minute customers; and the vegetable and fruit barrows were still out too, the hawkers in white coats yelling their wares and flapping their brownpaper packets, bringing prices down now that the day was ending. Around the bus-stop a crowd pushed and jostled to clamber onto the trackless trams, struggling against the passengers fighting to alight. Along the pavements little knots of youths lounged in twos and threes or more, watching the crowds streaming by, jeering, smoking, joking against the noise, under the balconies, in doorways, around the plate-glass windows. A half-mile of sound and movement and signs, signs, signs: Coca-Cola, Sale Now On, Jewellers, The Modern Outfitters, If You Don't Eat Here We'll Both Starve, Grand Picnic of Paradise Valley Luxury Buses, Teas, Coffee, Smoke, Have You Tried Our Milk Shakes, Billiard Club, The Rockingham Arms, Chine ... nce In Korea, Your Recommendation Is Our Advert, Dress Salon.

Michael Adonis moved idly along the pavement through the stream of people unwinding like a spool up the street. A music shop was playing shrill and noisy, 'Some of these days, you gonna miss me honey'; music from across the Atlantic, shipped in flat shellac discs to pound its jazz through the loudspeaker over the doorway.

He stopped outside the big plate window, looking in at the rows of guitars, banjoes, mandolins, the displayed gramophone parts, guitar picks, strings, electric irons, plugs, jews-harps, adaptors, celluloid dolls all the way from Japan, and the pictures of angels and Christ with a crown of thorns and drops of blood like lipstick marks on his pink forehead.

A fat man came out of the shop, his cheeks smooth and shiny with health, and said, 'You like to buy something, sir?'

'No man,' Michael Adonis said and spun his cigarette-end into the street where a couple of snot-nosed boys in ragged shirts and horny feet scrambled for it, pushing each other as they struggled to claim a few puffs.

Somebody said, 'Hoit, Mikey,' and he turned and saw the wreck of a youth who had fallen in beside him.

'Hullo, Joe.'

Joe was short and his face had an ageless quality about it under the grime, like something valuable forgotten in a junk shop. He had the soft brown eyes of a dog, and he smelled of a mixture of sweat, slept-in clothes and seaweed. His trousers had gone at the cuffs and knees, the rents held together with pins and pieces of string, and so stained and spotted that the original colour could not have been guessed at. Over the trousers he wore an ancient raincoat that reached almost to his ankles, the sleeves torn loose at the shoulders, the body hanging in ribbons, the front pinned together over his filthy vest. His shoes were worn beyond recognition.

Nobody knew where Joe came from, or anything about him. He just seemed to have happened, appearing in the District like a cockroach emerging through a floorboard. Most of the time he wandered around the harbour gathering fish discarded by fishermen and anglers, or along the beaches of the coast, picking limpets and mussels. He had a strange passion for things that came from the sea.

'How you, Joe?' Michael Adonis asked.

'Okay, Mikey.'

'What you been doing today?'

'Just strolling around the docks. York Castle came in this afternoon.'

'Ja?'

'You like mussels, Mikey? I'll bring you some.'

'That's fine, Joe.'

'I got a big starfish out on the beach yesterday. One big, big one. It was dead and stank.'

'Well, it's a good job you didn't bring it into town. City Council would be on your neck.'

'I hear they're going to make the beaches so only white people can go there,' Joe said.

'Ja. Read it in the papers. Damn sonsabitches.'

'It's going to get so's nobody can go nowhere.'

'I reckon so,' Michael Adonis said.

They were some way up the street now and outside the Queen Victoria. Michael Adonis said, 'You like a drink, Joe?' although he knew that the boy did not drink.

'No thanks, Mikey.'

'Well, so long.'

70

'So long, man.'

'You eat already?'

'Well ... no ... not yet,' Joe said, smiling humbly and shyly, moving his broken shoes gently on the rough cracked paving.

'Okay, here's a bob. Get yourself something. Parcel of fish and some chips.'

'Thanks, Mikey.'

'Okay. So long, Joe.'

'See you again.'

'Don't forget the mussels,' Michael Adonis said after him, knowing that Joe would forget anyway.

'I'll bring them,' Joe said, smiling back and raising his hand in a salute. He seemed to sense the other young man's doubt of his memory, and added a little fiercely, 'I won't forget. You'll see. I won't forget.'

Then he went up the street, trailing his tattered raincoat behind him like a sword-slashed, bullet-ripped banner just rescued from a battle.

Michael Adonis turned towards the pub and saw the two policemen coming towards him. They came down the pavement in their flat caps, khaki shirts and pants, their gun harness shiny with polish, and the holstered pistols heavy at their waists. They had hard, frozen faces as if carved out of pink ice, and hard, dispassionate eyes, hard and bright as pieces of blue glass. They strolled slowly and determinedly side by side, without moving off their course, cutting a path through the stream on the pavement like destroyers at sea.

They came on and Michael Adonis turned aside to avoid them, but they had him penned in with a casual, easy, skilful flanking manoeuvre before he could escape.

'*Waar loop jy rond, jong*? Where are you walking around, man?' The voice was hard and flat as the snap of a steel spring, and the one who spoke had hard, thin, chapped lips and a faint blonde down above them. He had flat cheekbones, 'pink-white, and thick, red-gold eyebrows and pale lashes. His chin was long and cleft and there was a small pimple beginning to form on one side of it, making a reddish dot against the pale skin.

'Going home,' Michael Adonis said, looking at the buckle of this policeman's belt. You learned from experience to gaze at some spot on their uniforms, the button of a pocket, or the bright smoothness of their Sam Browne belts, but never into their eyes, for that would be taken as an affront by them. It was only the very brave, or the very stupid, who dared look straight into the law's eyes, to challenge them or to question their authority.

The second policeman stuck his thumbs in his gun-belt and smiled distantly and faintly. It was more a slight movement of his lips, rather than a smile. The backs of his hands where they dropped over the leather of the belt were broad and white, and the outlines of the veins were pale blue under the skin, the skin covered with a field of tiny, slanting ginger-coloured hair. His fingers were thick and the knuckles big and creased and pink, the nails shiny and healthy and carefully kept.

This policeman asked in a heavy, brutal voice, 'Where's your dagga?'

'I don't smoke it.'

'Jong, turn out your pockets,' the first one ordered. 'Hurry up.'

Michael Adonis began to empty his pockets slowly, without looking up at them and thinking, with each movement, You mucking boers, you mucking boers. Some people stopped and looked and hurried on as the policemen turned the cold blue light of their eyes upon them. Michael Adonis showed them his crumbled and partly used packet of cigarettes, the money he had left over from his pay, a soiled handkerchief and an old piece of chewing gum covered with the grey fuzz from his pocket.

'Where did you steal the money?' The question was without humour, deadly serious, the voice topped with hardness like the surface of a file.

'Didn't steal it, baas (*you mucking boer*).'

'Well, muck off from the street. Don't let us find you standing around, you hear?'

'Yes, (*you mucking boer*).'

'Yes, what? who are you talking to, man?'

'Yes, baas (*You mucking bastard boer with your mucking gun and your mucking bloody red head*).'

They pushed past him, one of them brushing him aside with an elbow and strolled on. He put the stuff back into his pockets. And deep down inside him the feeling of rage, frustration and violence swelled like a boil, knotted with pain.

Notes

zol — a marijuana joint

dagga — marijuana

72

Rain

Richard Rive

Rain poured down, blotting out all sound with its sharp and vibrant tattoo. Dripping neon signs reflecting lurid reds and yellows in mirror-wet streets. Swollen gutters. Water overflowing and squelching onto pavements. Gurgling and sucking at storm-water drains. Table Mountain cut off by a grey film of mist and rain. A lost City Hall clock trying manfully to chime nine over an indifferent Cape Town. Baleful reverberations through a spluttering all-consuming drizzle.

Yellow light filters through from Solly's 'Grand Fish and Chips Palace'. Door tight-shut against the weather. Inside stuffy with heat, hot bodies, steaming clothes, and the nauseating smell of stale fish oil. Misty patterns on the plate-glass windows and a messy pool where rain has filtered beneath the door and mixed with the sawdust.

Solly himself in shirt sleeves, sweating, vulgar, and moody. Bellowing at a dripping woman who has just come in.

'Shut 'e damn door. Think you live in a tent?'

'Ag, Solly.'

'Don' ag me. You coloured people can never shut blarry doors.'

'Don't bloomingwell swear at me.'

'I bloomingwell swear at you, yes.'

'Come. Gimme two pieces 'e fish. Tail cut.'

'Two pieces 'e fish.'

'Raining like hell outside,' the woman said to no one.

'Mmmmmm. Raining like hell,' a thin befezzed Malay cut in.

'One an' six. Thank you. An' close 'e door behin' you.'

'Thanks. Think you got 'e on'y door in Hanover Street?'

'Go to hell!' Solly cut the conversation short and turned to another customer.

The north-wester sobbed heavy rain squalls against the window-panes. The Hanover Street bus screeched to a slithery stop and passengers darted for shelter in a cinema entrance. The street lamps shone blurredly.

Solly sweated as he wrapped parcels of fish and chips in a newspaper. Fish and chips. Vinegar? Wrap? One an' six please. Thank you! Next. Fish and chips. No? Two fish. No chips? Salt? Vinegar? One an' six please. Thank you! Next. Fish an' chips.

'Close 'e blarry door!' Solly glared daggers at a woman who had

73

just come in. She half-smiled apologetically at him.

'You coloured people are worse than Kaffirs.'

She struggled with the door and then stood dripping in a pool of wet sawdust. Solly left the counter to add two presto logs to the furnace. She moved out of the way. Another customer showed indignation at Solly's remark.

'You blooming Jews are always making coloured people out.'

'Go to hell!' Solly dismissed the attack on his race. Fish an' chips. Vinegar? Salt? One an' six. Thank you.

'Yes, madam?'

'Could you tell me when the bioscope comes out?'

'Am I the blooming manager?'

'Please.'

'Half pas' ten,' the Malay offered helpfully.

'Thank you. Can I stay here till then? It's raining outside.'

'I know it's blarrywell raining, but this is not a Salvation Army.'

'Please, baas!'

This caught Solly unawares. He had had his shop in that corner of District Six since most could remember and had been called a great many unsavoury things in the years. Solly didn't mind. But this caught him unawares. Please, baas. This felt good. His imagination adjusted a black bowtie to an evening suit. Please, baas.

'OK, stay for a short while. But when 'e rain stops you go!' She nodded dumbly and tried to make out the blurred name of the cinema opposite, through the misted windows.

'Waitin' fer somebody?' Solly asked. No response.

'I ask if yer waitin' fer somebody!' The figure continued to stare.

'Oh go to hell,' said Solly, turning to another customer.

Through the rain blur Siena stared at nothing in particular. Dim visions of slippery wet cars. Honking and wheezing in the rain. Spluttering buses. Heavy, drowsy voices in the Grand Fish and Chips Palace. Her eyes travelled beyond the street and the water cascades of Table Mountain, beyond the winter of Cape Town to the summer of the Boland. Past the green grapelands of Stellenbosch and Paarl and the stuffy wheat district of Malmesbury to the lazy sun and laughter of Teslaarsdal. A tired sun here. An uninterested sun. Now it seemed that the sun was weary of the physical effort of having to rise, to shine, to comfort, and to set.

Inside the nineteenth-century, gabled mission church she had first met Joseph. The church is still there, and beautiful, and the ivy climbs over it and makes it more beautiful. Huge silver oil lamps suspended from the roof, polished and shining. It was in the flicker of the lamps that she had first become aware of him. He was visiting from Cape Town. She sang that night like she had never sung before. Her favourite psalm.

'*All ging ik ook in een dal der schaduw des doods*' ... Though I walk through the valley of the shadow of death ... '*der schaduw des doods.*' And then he had looked at her. Everyone had looked at her, for she was good in solos.

'*Ik zoude geen kwaad vreezen*' ... I will fear no evil. And she had not feared, but loved. Had loved him. Had sung for him. For the wide eyes, the yellow skin, the high cheekbones. She had sung for a creator who could create a man like Joseph. '*Want gij zijt met mij; Uw stok en Uw staf, die vertroosten mij.*'

Those were black and white polka-dot nights when the moon did a golliwog cakewalk across a banjo-strung sky. Nights of sweet remembrances when he had whispered love to her and told her of Cape Town. She had giggled coyly at his obscenities. It was fashionable, she hoped, to giggle coyly at obscenities. He lived in one of those streets off District Six and was, he boasted, quite a one among the girls. She heard of Molly and Miena and Sophia and a sophisticated Charmaine, who was almost a schoolteacher and always spoke English. But he told her that he had only found love in Teslaarsdal. She wasn't sure whether to believe him. And then he had felt her richness and the moon darted behind a cloud.

The loud screeching of the train to Cape Town. Screeching loud enough to drown the protest of her family. The wrath of her father. The icy stares of Teslaarsdal matrons. Loud and confused screechings to drown her hysteria, her ecstasy. Drowned and confused in the roar of a thousand cars and a hundred thousand lights and a summer of carnival evenings that are Cape Town. Passion in a tiny room off District Six. Desire surrounded by four bare walls and a rickety chair and a mounted cardboard tract that murmured *Bless this House*.

And the agony of the nights when he came home later and later and sometimes not at all. The waning of his passion and whispered names of others. Molly and Miena and Sophia. Charmaine. The helpless knowledge that he was slipping from her. Faster and faster. Gathering momentum.

'Not that I'm saying so but I only heard ...'

'Why don't you go to bioscope one night and see for yourself ...'

'Marian's man is searching for Joseph ...' Searching for Joseph. Looking for Joseph. Knifing for Joseph. Joseph. Joseph! JOSEPH! Molly! Miena! Sophia! Names! Names! Names! Gossip. One-sided desire. Go to bioscope and see. See what? See why? When! Where!

And after he had been away a week she decided to see. Decided

to go through the rain and stand in a sweating fish and chips shop
owned by a blaspheming Jew. And wait for the cinema to come out.
The rain had stopped sobbing against the plate-glass window. A
skin-soaking drizzle now set in. Continous. Unending. Filming
everything with dark depression. A shivering, weeping neon sign
flickered convulsively on and off. A tired Solly shot a quick glance
at a cheap alarm clock.

'Half pas' ten, bioscope out soon.'

Siena looked more intently through the misty screen. No movement
whatsoever in the deserted cinema foyer.

'Time it was bloomingwell out.' Solly braced himself for the wave
of after-show customers who would invade his Palace.

'Comin' out late tonight, missus.'

'Thank you, baas.'

Solly rubbed sweat out of his eyes and took in her neat and plain
figure. Tired face but good legs. A few late stragglers catching colds
in the streets. Wet and squally outside.

'Your man in bioscope?'

She was intent on a khaki-uniformed usher struggling to open the
door.

'Man in bioscope, missus?'

The cinema had to come out some time or other. An usher
opening the door, adjusting the outside gate. Preparing for the
crowds to pour out. Vomited and spilled out.

'Man in bioscope?'

No response.

'Oh, go to hell!'

They would be out now. Joseph would be out. She rushed for the
door, throwing words of thanks to Solly.

'Close 'e blarry door!'

She never heard him. The drizzle had stopped. An unnatural calm
hung over the empty foyer, over the deserted street. Over her
empty heart. She took up her stand on the bottom step. Expectantly.
Her heart pounding.

Then they came. Pouring, laughing, pushing, jostling. She stared
with fierce intensity, but faces passed too fast. Laughing, roaring,
gay. Wide-eyed, yellow-skinned, high-cheekboned. Black, brown,
ivory, yellow. Black-eyed, laughing-eyed, gay, bouncing. No Joseph.
Palpitating heart that felt like bursting into a thousand pieces. If she
should miss him. She found herself searching for the wrong face.
Solly's face. Ridiculously searching for hard blue eyes and a sharp
white chin in a sea of ebony and brown. Solly's face. Missing half a
hundred faces and then again searching for the familiar high cheek-

76

bones. Solly. Joseph. Molly. Miena. Charmaine.

The drizzle restarted. Studying overcoats instead of faces. Longing for the pale blue shirt she had seen in the shop at Solitaire. A bargain at one pound, five shillings. She had scraped and scrounged to buy it for him. A week's wages. Collecting her thoughts and continuing the search for Joesph. And then the thinning out of the crowd and the last few stragglers. The ushers shutting the iron gates. They might be shutting Joseph in. Herself out. Only the ushers left. And the uncompromising iron gates.

'Please, is Joseph inside?'

'Who's Joseph?'

'Is Joseph still inside?'

'Joseph who?'

They were teasing her. Laughing behind her back. Preventing her from finding him.

'Joseph is inside!' she shouted frenziedly.

'Look, merrim, it's raining cats an' dogs. Go home.'

Go home. To whom? To what? An empty room? An empty bed? A tract that shrieked its lie, *Bless this House?*'

And then she was aware of the crowd on the corner. Maybe he was there. Running and peering into every face. Joseph. The crowd in the drizzle. Two battling figures. Joseph. Figures locked in struggle slithering in the wet gutter. Muck streaking down clothes through which wet bodies were silhouetted. Joseph. A blue shirt. And then she wiped the rain out of her eyes and saw him. Fighting for his life. Desperately kicking in the gutter. Joseph. The blast of a police whistle. A pickup van screeching to a stop.

'Please, sir, it wasn't him. They all ran away. Please, sir, he's Joseph. He done nothing. He done nothing, my baas. Please, sir, he's my Joseph. Please, baas!'

'Maak dat jy weg kom. Get away. Voetsak!'

'Please, sir, it wasn't him. They ran away!'

Alone. An empty bed. An empty room.

Solly's Grand Fish and Chips Palace crowded out. People milling inside. Rain once more squalling and sobbing against the door and windows. Swollen gutters unable to cope with the giddy rush of water. Solly sweating to deal with the after-cinema rush.

Fish an' chips. Vinegar? Salt? One an' six. Thank you. Sorry, no fish. Wait five minutes. Chips on'y. Vinegar? Ninepence. Tickey change. Thank you. Sorry, no fish. Five minutes' time. Chips? Ninepence. Thank you. Solly paused for breath and stirred the fish.

'What's trouble outside?'

'Bioscope, Solly.'

'No, man, outside!'

'I say, bioscope.'

'What were 'e police doin'? Sorry, no fish yet, sir. Five minutes' time. What were 'e police doin'?'

'A fight in 'e blooming rain.'

'Jeeesus, in 'e rain?'

'Ja.'

'Who was fightin'?'

'Joseph an' somebody.'

'Joseph?'

'Ja, fellow in Arundel Street.'

'Yes, I know Joseph. Always in trouble. Chucked him outta here a'reddy.'

'Well, that chap.'

'An' who?'

'Dinno.'

'Police got them?'

'Got Joseph.'

'Why were 'ey fightin'? Fish in a minute, sir.'

'Over a dame.'

'Who?'

'You know Miena who works by Patel? Now she. Her boyfriend caught 'em.'

'In bioscope?'

'Ja.'

Solly chuckled deeply, suggestively.

'See that woman an' 'e police?'

'What woman?'

'Dame cryin' to 'e police.'

'They say it's Joseph's dame.'

'Joseph always got plenty 'e dames. F-I-S-H − R-E-A-D-Y!!! Two pieces for you, sir? One an' six. Shilling change. Fish an' chips? One an' six. Thank you. Fish on'y? Vinegar? Salt? Ninepence. Tickey change. Thank you!'

'What you say about e' woman?'

'They say Joseph's girl was crying to 'e police.'

'Oh, he got plenty 'e girls.'

'This one was living with him.'

'Oh, what she look like? Fish, sir?'

'O.K. Nice legs.'

'Hmmmmm,' said Solly. 'Hey, close 'e damn door. Oh, you again.' Siena came in. A momentary silence. Then a buzzing and whispering.

'Oh,' said Solly, nodding as someone whispered over the counter to him. 'I see. She was waiting here. Musta been waitin' for him.' A young girl in jeans giggled.

'Fish an' chips costs one an' six, madam.'

'Wasn't it one an' three before?'

'Before the Boer war, madam. Price of fish go up. Potatoes go up an' you expect me to charge one an' three?'

'Why not?'

'Oh, go to hell! Next, please!'

'Yes, that's 'e one Solly.'

'Mmmm. Excuse me, madam' — turning to Siena — 'like some fish an' chips? Free of charge, never min' 'e money.'

'Thank you, my baas.'

The rain now sobbed wildly as the shop emptied, and Solly counted the cash in his till. Thousands of watery horses charging down the street. Rain drilling into cobbles and pavings. Miniature waterfalls down the sides of buildings. Blurred lights through unending streams. Siena listlessly holding the newspaper parcel of fish and chips.

'You can stay here till it clears up,' said Solly.

She looked up tearfully.

Solly grinned, showing his yellow teeth. 'It's quite OK.'

A smile flickered across her face for a second.

'It's quite OK by me.'

She looked down and hesitated for a moment. Then she struggled against the door. It yielded with a crash and the north-wester howled into Solly's Palace.

'Close 'e blarry door!' he said, grinning.

'Thank you, my baas,' she said as she shivered out into the rain.

Paradise

Achmat Dangor

> Oh paradise,
> cool paradise of Africa
> your sea roars
> like the restless roots
> of our lives

and yet does not give life
to the dreams
of the people
you have forgotten.

Here, around me,
they destroy my city.
district Six,
they dismantle you
    stone by stone
rock of my history.

On the walls
of my last refuge
cockroaches run
secretive and quiet,
an omen:
love and hope
that will have to
be hidden in darkness.

Somewhere in the twilight
a banjo trills, somewhere
on an overgrown terrace
people sing and people laugh,
the human voices of everyday.

Oh paradise, cool paradise
of Africa,
what memories you recreate.

Oh why, why do you
tighten the chains?

Home

Dan Pillay

Row upon endless row of houses. They reach out, stretching toward
the horizon. When they have touched it, I look down upon my
phalanx of concrete soldiers standing to attention, and salute their

perfect uniformity. Each is an exact replica of its neighbours; their ranks are unmarred by differences in size, structure, design ... no, my clones are quite perfect ... except for one minor mutation. Each is painted in its own shade of hideousness, lurid exlamations of variety. My soldiers' skins are all of different colours — perhaps it's part of the National Party's new reform policy — multi-racialism.

Between this meticulous monotony, this anonymous uniformity, stand pathetic efforts of enterprise and ingenuity — 'improved' properties. Pseudo-Spanish facades clumsily grafted onto their ashamed frontages, these bastardized monuments proudly leer their 'superiority'. Are you perhaps impressed by the enterprise, the ingenuity of our hardworking masses? Knock at a door. Go on! Ask Madam if you may use the toilet. Go on! It's not so unusual here. Why is Madam suddenly so flustered, so embarrassed? Aha! Behold the mark of Cain! The outside toilet — nightmare of our enterprising home-owners. Yes, it is a constant source of exasperation to them that, no matter how transformed the new house may be, the outside toilet will remain an irritating reminder of the 'council house' stigma.

Chatsworth — the Indian Soweto. Welcome to my home.

Bus at last! Driver tries to run me down. I dive for the pavement, hurling a torrent of verbal abuse and sputum in his direction. It is Seela — he used to drive me to school when I was just six. Hasn't forgotten me though, despite Waterford, and despite the fact that we've both aged somewhat — him more than me.

'Hey brazzo! Who do you think you are, jolling in the road, huh?'

The usual banter — he will josh me about my accent, and in retaliation, I will do my famous impersonation of the typical Durban bus-driver. He's very impressed because I'm in a private school.

'With vet-ous?!' he demands, eyes wide with disbelief. For the nth time, I confirm this. 'Yassus! And vet-stukkies too?!' and he winks and leers. Accordingly, I will wink and leer as well, and he will end with the usual pertinent comment, 'Ah, what the fok! Cherries are all the same underneath anyway!'

There is no reply to his rhetorical statement, so I simply smile sagely. He offers me a cigarette. Rothmans, blue pack — *the* brand in Durban. I accept — to refuse would be a gross infringement of our ritual, an insult.

Bus starts up, lurching across broken ground like the driver on a Friday night, then gathers speed as it roars down the hill at breakneck speed. Speedy Gonzales performs his usual stunt of bringing the bus to a screaming halt as he virtually stands on the brake-pedal. It is at this moment that I usually remember my fervent vow of the last holiday never to travel on Seela's bus again. One day he'll kill me.

The other passengers, mainly old, withered ladies and bored house-wives seem to be of the same opinion. Their exchange of scandal, rumour, recipes, and weddings/funerals/births are continually inter-rupted as the bus ferociously tears its way through the narrow roads. After some manoeuvring, I find myself in a fairly safe, comfortable position, and proceed to dream, perchance to sleep.

A couple tie themselves into an inextricable love-knot in front of me. She is playing truant from school. He is unemployed, a thug, a tsotsi, but with all the glamour of not being a mere schoolboy, backed up by the uneasy repution of his status as a township gangster. They will go to the movies, the 'bioscope' — the 10 am show at the Avalon, Shiraz, or perhaps Isfahan, if he is in the money. Outside the theatre, he will tease, and she will giggle. Inside the theatre, she will whisper sentiments of undying love and sincerity as she tenderly caresses his hair with her lips; with the same intensity, he will snort passionate mixtures of saliva and snot and desire down her throat, biting, sucking, chewing, until she is choked by his love and phlegm. During the movie, she will eat popcorn. He will eat her. After the movie, probably in good old African bush, he will screw her, and, with her new-found love, she will be escorted home. And tomorrow, when she is marked 'present' at school, another girl will be marked 'absent'.

The spice of life is variety . . .

While I have been thinking these scandalous thoughts, the maniac at the wheel has managed to bring us to the outskirts of the city. We charge merrily through a series of unblinking, red traffic-lights, avoiding possible accidents, evading irate drivers, and swerve around the final bend; an old woman with a whiter-than-usual face and an upside-down bowl of cherries on her head scurries back to the pavement as we sweep through yet another robot. I shut my eyes firmly — seeing is believing, so I'd prefer not to see it — I sleep — somehow.

A sudden, bone-jarring impetus that raises me to my knees, combined with a banshee-like wail from the overworked brakes, serves to inform me that Seela has 'braked' with his usual flair and expertise, and we have arrived safely.

Durban — clean, White, commercial, department-store Durban and squalid, dirty, small-business Durban — the Indian quarter. The Indian quarter — a more respectable area with high-fashion clothing-stores, bazaars, and restaurants for the élite, and a more disreputable sector, where anything from an illegal and unsterile abortion to an illegal and very sterile switch-blade may be procured. The Indian quarter — harsh traffic-smoke from exhaust-pipes mingled with that unmistakable reek from dagga-pipes; over it all, the pungent tingle of mystic Oriental spices.

Traffic swarms down the streets. With the easy nonchalance of the street-wise, I stroll across. Newspaper-vendor on the corner exhorts people to 'Readallaboutit! Post!' For a carelessly tossed twenty-cent piece, I read about the latest murders and rapes and briefly pause to admire the arthritic 'model' reclining against the page, before casually tossing her into a convenient rubbish-bin.

Hundreds of scurrying humans, Black, Indian, Coloured − here and there, a splash of uneasy White. Swaggering six abreast, a bunch of tsotsis, self-appointed town-toughs clad in the regulation uniform of scrubbed, white 'Onitsuka' sneakers, faded 'Lee' jeans, white T-shirts, black 'Tiger' jackets turned inside-out, cheese-kops crowned with baseball caps. Pseudo-toughs, hyenas who fight only with the pack. People melt away from their contaminated path. Face to face. Dark anonymous glances behind dark anonymous glasses rake over me. I shrink into a shop-window and display extreme interest in sets of seductive-looking lingerie. Smarmy shop-assistant appears with the look usually reserved for queers. I grin sheepishly, before disappearing rapidly down the nearest alley.

Down the alley, I must evade the sincere advances of a greasy, sharp-faced rat, who begs me to buy his mother's 'genwyne eighteen-carat gold ring, I swear, my broer!' while a mere 'Get stuffed' suffices to return a crestfallen seller of 'real Swiss watches' to his lair.

Gorgeous silk saris in store-windows, heavy with gold filigree and rich, intricate embroidery; woman brushes past me − my head swims with Eastern scent, Western perfume and the faint, gentle aura of sandalwood soap. The cloying taint of incense from the opulence of the store adds to all this olfactory excitement.

On a deserted corner, shifty, red-eyed rooker drags surreptitiously on a zol. I decline the doped generosity of the held-out joint, shake off the grimy envelope of 'DP' being pressed into my palm. A well-rounded nubile lip-licking bruinmeisie sways beckoning hips at me − for five rand, I can accept a semen-stained mattress in a run-down apartment on Queen Street, the promise of warm, foetid, sweat-wet thighs, and the shuddering, heaving gasps of her sham orgasm. Sorry, honey.

The flash of gleaming stainless steel and the evil click! of a pent-up switch-blade reveals a bullet-headed tsotsi. Panicky glances around, the squeeze of terror tightening in my throat. Click! Disappearance of blade, haft quickly concealed under a sweaty palm. Menace and malice twinkle in the grin of brown, rotten teeth.

'Flick-knife, broer, genwyne American import, ek sê my broer . . .'
Get stuffed.

Dozens of fat, old, Black women selling fruit, vegetables, beer, roasted mealies. Portable herbalists, wares prominently displayed on cardboard boxes, offer remedies for every conceivable ailment. Evil-smelling brown mixtures of magic in 'Mainstay' bottles. Get stuffed. The raucous singing of gospel songs from a devout 'choir' of beggars. The few cents thrown down in front of them disappear dexterously into the 'blind' beggar's pockets. Brown coins for brown people.

Suddenly, the casual hubbub is shattered into a whirlwind of movement. Women running, loads still balanced on spiky heads with the inimitable grace of the African woman. Our omnipotent herbalist healers are dwindling into the distance, bottles of magic foregotten in their haste. The gospel singing abruptly collapses, hymns suddenly punctuated by panicky shouts, and the beggars, clutching their coppers, flee towards the sanctuary of a crowded bus-terminal. Scattered on the ground, beer-cans, fruit, bottles, mealies. The white patrol-van noses its way delicately through the throng, before easing to a halt. There are few Blacks around now; just Coloureds and Indians. Apprehensive Black faces tightened in fear, apprehensive Black fingers tightened around passes. Door opens. Big, heavy-bellied White cop, dark glasses and two lines of big, white teeth bisecting his florid face. He carefully and unhurriedly collects fruit, mealies, beercans, packs them into the van, and, fangs bared in a grimace of a grin, settles himself into the driver's seat. Large damp patches under his arms − evidence of Durban heat and hard work, no doubt. Duty calls. . . the van disappears.

Slowly, life returns to normal; the grating melancholy of toneless hymns, the pompous proclamations of the herbalists, and the high-pitched cries of the fruit-sellers.

Lunch − I will dine today at Kapitan's Vegetarian Restaurant. The Kapitan − a fascinating place. For a rand, a thick, china bowl of curry and several pieces of bread are yours. Cracked glasses of tepid water are on the house. Women and children are relegated to a quiet corner, so that the men may eat in peace and engage in important discussions. Kapitan's is devoid of any class barrier. Executives clad in grey three-piece suits hob-nob with sweat-stained labourers in overalls; as they eat, they pore over the card for next week's horseraces at Greyville, earnestly debating the merits of jockeys and horses.

The cafè is crowded to capacity − as usual. I will have to sit at the tsotsis' table. They grudgingly give way and, clutching my bowl, my bread, my bottle of Coca-Cola, I collapse into a rickety old chair. Kapitan's is not exactly a restaurant — it is a sleazy, run-down, dilapidated cafè, not too dirty (by local standards!), but with good food. Along one wall runs a counter where one orders one's food. Below the cash register sits a sleek, black, carefully-oiled pistol and, on a convenient shelf, a sjambok and several knobkieries are in evidence. Most regular customers are aware of these facts — that is why there is seldom a fight in the Kapitan. The rest of the place is crowded with cheap, orange, plastic tables, cheap, orange, plastic chairs, and cheap, brown, plastic people.

My bread has disappeared — probably down one of my companions' throats. I look around — four sardonic grins, four pairs of dark glasses follow my movements. Rigid with helpless anger and impotence, I get up and claw my way to the counter for more bread. When I have fought my way back to the table, followed by a volley of oaths from irritated diners, I am greeted by the grin of an empty Coca-Cola bottle, and the mocking stare of my white, cleaned china bowl. I have lost my appetite.

Dawdling along the streets again, warmed by a sleepy sun. From the mosque, the undulating wail of the muezzin reminds the population that it is Friday and signals the closing of dozens of stores. Scores of Muslims, topped in white, finely-woven skull-caps thread their way hurriedly towards the vast conglomerate of onion domes and minarets, devoted mice lured by a holy Pied Piper

Deserted streets, a few dedicated window-shoppers, someone hurrying to lunch, the occasional Muslim late for his prayers. For an hour the sudden, ghostly quiet will remain, interrupted only by the few passers-by, the now almost-silent trickle of traffic, the whisper of litter swept along the streets by the wind. Then, hunger satisfied, pious obligations completed, stores will re-open, the streets will teem with the rush of humanity, the clamour of commerce and the tornado of traffic will drown us out; as I approach the bus-terminal, I am filled with dismay and horror as I recognise the driver of my bus — it is Seela.

Notes

brazzo — an elaboration of 'bra', an abbreviation of 'brother', much used in black urban townships as a friendly address

jolling — 'to jol' is a verb with many meanings; here it would mean 'walking, playing, messing about'

vet-ous — mispronunciation of Afrikaans: 'wit ous', white boys

vet-stukkies — literally 'white pieces', ie girls

cherries — another slang term for girls

cheese-kop — Afrikaans: 'kop' is head, hence 'shaved heads'
broer — Afrikaans: brother
rooker — Afrikaans: smoker, usually of marijuana
zol — marijuana joint
DP — a good brand of marijuana, 'Durban Poison'
bruinmeisie — Afrikaans: brown girl
ek sê — Afrikaans: I say

Living in a Flat in Eldorado Park

Fhazel Johennesse

twenty-two kilometres away from the city
perpetually ravaged by wind and dust
the roads bumpy and a challenge
to all car owners and the postal service
a happy lackadaisical affair and
the blocks of flats scattered around at random
and the outside walls to the flats defying
cleanliness and the parade of life
outside my door:
the drunk trying to mount the steps
swearing as he skids in predecessors' vomit
and a curious two-year-old watching
his antics and a woman of indeterminate age
dragging an impossible bundle of washing with half a
dozen kids clawing at her skirs and another
toddler searching for space on a wall
to mark his passing with a piece of chalk
and the occasional tinkle of glass
as a stone is hurled through a window
and the grating calling of a mother
shouting for her child and
the rich pong of gas exuding from
the slowly rotting garbage in dustbins
and the throaty gurgle of pipes
as someone else's crap passes through
my flat and the infuriating
tap tap tap on the ceiling as
some brat upstairs explores the
mysteries of his floor with a hammer

and the frequent knock on the door
as someone tries yet again to sell
tomatoes steelwool washing baskets
dance-tickets spices or toilet-seats
and the maddening toot-toot of
the milkman as he sells his milk
for four cents more than the dairy does

i think of all these things
when someone asks me if i like living
in eldorado park
not bad
i say
not bad at all

Make Like Slaves

Richard Rive

A PLAY FOR RADIO

> *fx: Fade in Missa Luba. Knock on door. There is no response and knocking is repeated through the music.*

HE: [*quietly on mic*] Come in.

> *fx: Knocking repeated*

HE: [*shouts*] Come in!

> *fx: Door opens*

HE: Oh! Hallo.

> *fx: Door shuts*

SHE: [*coming on mic*] Surprised to see me? I said I would come and I came. I'm sure you never dreamt that we would meet again after disembarking from that dreadful ship.

HE: Yes, it really is a surprise. Please do sit down. Let me take these books out of the way. I'm afraid there are no other chairs. Have mine, I can sit on the bed. Let me take off this record.

SHE: Please don't. It's beautiful, the music. What's it called?

HE: Missa Luba. Know it? A Congolese Mass. Please, do sit.

SHE: It's so exciting. Sophisticated and unsophisticated at the same time.

HE: Yes, that's true. Do let me switch it off though, otherwise we can't speak!

fx: The music stops

HE: That's better. Now we can hear ourselves. Music has to be listened to or not listened to. I don't believe in talking through music.

SHE: You must let me come again and listen to it. Missa Luba you say? It would certainly suit my play.

HE: Yes, you must come again — if you don't mind the state of my room.

SHE: I don't really mind. [*pause*] I suppose you're wondering why I'm here.

HE: Well, I dare say your arrival is somewhat unexpected.

SHE: The last time we spoke was just before we got off the ship in Cape Town.

HE: I remember.

SHE: I said I would see you again, if I had some difficulty. You know the things we spoke about the last evening.

HE: That was almost a year ago.

SHE: More than a year ago Unfortunately I am in a terrible hurry now. I have to be off to a drama group I run in the African location. I have to be there by eight. I'm running into a bit of difficulty with them and need your advice. Heard of the Nyanga Players?

HE: Yes, I think I've read ...

SHE: I don't think so. Very few people know about them, but they will soon, at least I hope so. One of the consulates in town has asked me to put on an indigenous play for their staff. They want Blacks since they also have their own Negroes back home. Does one say Blacks or Africans? I'm never sure.

HE: Suit yourself.

SHE: I thought about it for a few weeks, a play I mean, and came up with a rather good idea.

HE: Yes?

SHE: The slavery story. It neatly straddles their continent and ours. You seem bored. Want to hear more?

HE: I'm sorry, I don't mean to be rude. Do go on.

SHE: The first act is set in Africa. They sing indigenous African songs. You should hear my Nyanga Players. The throb of the primitive. Dancing and rhythm. Palm-fronds and jungle drums. Africa.

HE: Continue.

SHE: If you're interested. Act two is literally and dramatically the centre. The middle passage. They are captured and in a boat going across the Atlantic. An overcrowded boat. Chained down, whipped, abused. The longing for home. Nostalgia. Have you read Robert Hayden? I believe he is a famous American Negro poet. I came across him very recently. He wrote a beautiful epic about it called *Middle Passage*. I would like to call my play *Middle Passage* if Mr Hayden doesn't mind.

HE: I've read Robert Hayden.

SHE: I do like him.

HE: What about your play? You were describing act two.

SHE: And then the finale. They make like slaves.

HE: What?

SHE: They make like slaves. Oh, it's a bit of drama school slang I picked up when I was studying in London. They make like slaves. They sing sorrow-songs. Spirituals. This can be very moving.

HE: 'Yet do I marvel.'

SHE: Excuse me?

HE: I was quoting from another great American poet, Countee Cullen.

SHE: Was he also a Negro?

HE: I don't think it matters. He was a poet. 'Yet do I marvel at this curious thing, to make a poet black and bid him sing.'
    Pause

SHE: That really has feeling. How do they say? Soul.

HE: Yes, it has feeling.

SHE: But this is actually what I came about. I'm having some problems with my players.

HE: Problems?

SHE: Yes. To give you one example. I'm strict, very strict when it comes to work. Especially about things like punctuality. I think they resent it. I think they also resent the fact that I am white and they are black.

HE: So, how do I come into this?

SHE: Well ... You're in the middle so to speak. Being brown you can speak to them and to me. They'll understand. I'll understand. They'll listen to you. I'd like to tell you more but I'm afraid I just have to go now otherwise I'll be late. I'd like to come around next week and explain it all to you. May I?

HE: I don't really know.

SHE: Please say yes. I do need your advice. What about next Thursday evening? May I come early? At six? The rehearsal is at eight.

HE: But I won't be able to feed ...

SHE: Don't worry about that. I'll pick you up here, and you can have a bite at my flat, and maybe, if you're not too busy you can go to the rehearsal with me afterwards. You must be quite frank. Don't spare me anything.

HE: Well, all right ... I think next Thursday...

SHE: At six? That'll be first class [*going off mic*] I'll pick you up here. I really must be off to Nyanga now. I like the Missa Luba and that Countee Cullen man. Till Thursday then. Bye now.

fx: Door opens

HE: Good-bye.

fx: Door shuts. Short pause

HE: [*softly*] What the hell.

fx: Missa Luba is suddenly turned on full blast

HE: What the hell. [*loudly*] What the bloody hell!

fx: Peak music and then fade out

fx: Fade in Missa Luba. Knock on door

HE: [*above the music*] Come in!

fx: Knock repeated

HE: Who is it! Come in!

fx: Door opens

HE: Oh hell! Let me first switch this damn thing off.

fx: Music stops abruptly

HE: Oh ... Good evening. Come in. I'm sorry if I sounded unpleasant but you took me by surprise. I must have sounded very abrupt.

SHE: [*coming in on mic*] You sound as though you hadn't expected me.

HE: Yes.

SHE: Well? What does *yes* mean? You expected me or not?

HE: To tell the truth not really.

SHE: It's Thursday evening. We had an appointment for tonight. Or shall I remind you? I was to pick you up more than an hour ago for supper at my flat, and then, if you could manage you would go with me to Nyanga.

90

HE: Of course. Yes, of course. Hell, I'm sorry about this. Pity you didn't phone me earlier this evening to remind me.

SHE: I did. I tried four times between six and now, but it must be rather difficult for you to hear it ringing especially when it's off its rest.

HE: Yes, how silly of me. I normally take the phone off when I'm working. Breaks my concentration when it rings. All noise disturbs me then.

SHE: Is that why you were playing Missa Luba somewhat loudly?

HE: I give up. I'm sorry about all this. I clean forgot about tonight.

SHE: Quite sure?

HE: Yes, I'm sure. Don't you believe me? I forgot.

SHE: People sometimes forget because it's convenient. You have plenty of work this evening?'

HE: To tell the truth ... hell, I know it sounds lame ... Yes, I've been so immersed in work these last few days that I've forgotten about the rest of the world, forgotten people and appointments. But I will certainly come if it's not already too late.

SHE: It's not too late.

HE: Then I'll come. What exactly is it you want me to do? You haven't really explained the nature of the problem.

SHE: Well, I am here because I need help, your help. If you can manage to come I shall indeed be grateful. And if you would like some supper afterwards to recover, it is waiting at my flat.

HE: I'm not so sure about the supper afterwards, but I shall certainly come now. I think I would like to get back fairly early and continue with my work.

SHE: Continue with it now. Don't let me disturb you. We can always discuss my problems some other time. When you're not too busy.

HE: I understand how you're feeling.

SHE: [going off mic] Well then, I'll see you some time.

HE: Wait. I said I'd come with you.

SHE: [off mic] This evening?

HE: I'll come this evening. What time does the rehearsal start?

SHE: [coming on mic] Eight. I don't want to be late. It's only seven now. We have a bit of time to spare.

HE: Then relax. Have a seat. Like a drink to calm your nerves? I'm really sorry ...

SHE: Look, if it's inconvenient for you I'd rather you stayed at home and went on with your work. I can manage tonight on my own. I'll give you a ring during the week if your phone is not off the hook. I'm sorry to have involved you.

HE: I know this sounds awkward, but I repeat that I forgot about

91

this evening. You must take my word for it, I forgot. Now I'm prepared to come along whether you find me useful or not. I'll come.

SHE: Well ... if you insist. Then I think we had better be going, I'll explain in the car.

HE: [*going off mic*] In a moment. Let me get my coat.

SHE: Are you quite sure you want to come?'

HE: [*coming back on mic*] Yes, I'm quite sure. O.K. I'm ready now.

SHE: [*going off mic*] You do seem to be forgetful.

HE: [*going off mic*] What do you mean?

SHE: You've forgotten our drink.

HE: Damn. So I have. I really am cracking up. [*laughs*]

fx: Door opens

To forget a drink ... I am really cracking up.

fx: Door slams shut
fx: Fade in. Sound of a car being driven. Gears change. The gears stick in third, then after what seems like a struggle, it changes to top and then the engine runs smoothly

SHE: I'm sorry to have taken you from your work like this, but I wouldn't have done it if I hadn't really needed your help for this rehearsal.

HE: Yes.

SHE: I really must have this car seen to. Notice how the third gear sticks. Know anything about gears?

HE: No.

SHE: As I was saying, I must apologize for having dragged you away from your work on an evening like this. I know how important your work is to you.

HE: It's all right.

SHE: What were you doing when I knocked? Marking essays or writing? I bet you were writing poetry.

HE: I was writing.

SHE: You must tell me what you are working on. I am interested in your career, I really am. Not everyone can write. I'm sure you will become my favourite poet.

HE: Yes.

SHE: Have you been published much?

HE: No.

SHE: Regret having come? You don't sound very talkative. Yes, I'm sorry about dragging you away. I am sure you were working on something big. One day you'll prove a credit ...

HE: To what?

SHE: To ... Oh, I know it sounds dripping wet and sugary — sometimes I feel ashamed of being white, of sounding patronizing. But you will prove a credit to ...

HE: To my people?

SHE: There now, you said it, not me. Yes, if you put it that way, to your people.

HE: To the coloured people. To two million brown South Africans. And maybe a few million Blacks thrown in.

SHE: That's not what I mean.

HE: That's what *I* mean.

SHE: Am I driving too fast for you?

HE: No.

SHE: I *am* driving too fast.

HE: If you prefer it.

SHE: But it's important for us to get to the location on time. I can't afford to arrive late at the rehearsal, after telling them so often that they are not punctual.

HE: Can't set a bad example.

SHE: Yes, in a way. I don't know why it is, and I don't want you to misunderstand me, but Africans are never on time.

HE: A very bad racial characteristic.

SHE: No, I don't mean it in that way. I am only speaking in terms of my own experience. I have not been to a single rehearsal since I've started in Nyanga and found everyone there on time.

HE: There must be reasons.

SHE: I'm sure there are. But just you wait and see. We are right now breaking our necks to get there on time, and we'll find maybe one or two waiting.

HE: Are brown people also not punctual?

SHE: You're being cruel.

HE: And Whites?

SHE: I think you're being very unfair.

HE: Are Whites punctual?

SHE: If you want an answer, some are and some are not.

HE: And you are the punctual kind?

SHE: Please, I don't want us to quarrel. I'm trying my best to help in my small way. It's not my fault that I am of a different colour. I try and treat all the same. I like all people.

HE: Except?

SHE: Except what ...?

HE: Except unpunctual Blacks?

SHE: You don't mean that, do you?

HE: No, I don't think so. I'm sorry. I'm bad company. I'm feeling like hell. My mind is still on my work. One ought to be able to laugh about some things sometimes.

SHE: One ought. [*giggles*] If you're white, you're never late.

HE: If you're brown, after eight.

SHE: But if you're black ... [*they both laugh*]

HE: [*suddenly*] Hell, stop.

fx: Car skids to an abrupt halt then moves off again

HE: Didn't you see that traffic cop?

SHE: No, I didn't. Better watch out I suppose. I will have to keep my foot down nevertheless, we haven't much time.

HE: Play it cool. You don't need to prove your punctuality.

SHE: I should have let you drive.

HE: Maybe.

SHE: I am sure you're a better driver than me.

HE: Yes, maybe.

SHE: Are you a good driver?

HE: [*tensely*] I can't drive.

fx: Fade out car
fx: Fade in car taking a corner, then picking up speed again

HE: Yes, so it took more than a year for us to meet again. Sorry to interrupt the conversation, but I seem to have run out of cigarettes.

SHE: Have one of mine. There's an open packet in the cubby.

fx: Rummaging in cubby — packet opened

HE: Light one for you?

SHE: Please.

fx: Match is struck

SHE: Thanks. Why only one? Aren't you smoking?

HE: Much as I'd like to, I can't stand menthol.

SHE: I'm sorry about that. I'll stop as soon as we can get to a shop. Sure you won't have menthol in the meanwhile?

HE: Quite sure.

SHE: I feel bad about smoking while you're not.

HE: Don't let it upset you. You were speaking about the Nyanga Players before we were so rudely interrupted.

SHE: I was saying that I seemed to sense a touch of resentment towards me from the first time I went.

HE: How come you went in the first place?

94

SHE: I went because I wanted to help. After I arrived from England, shall I say after *we* arrived from England, I felt I had to do something for the under-privileged. I wanted to help the people who needed it.

HE: So you gave them drama. Why?

SHE: What do you mean, why?

HE: Why people like them?

SHE: Surely I don't need to explain. You must understand. They needed some form of assistance and they have talent. They are born actors.

HE: Like the French are born lovers, the Italians born singers, the Jews ...

SHE: I'm not saying that. All I'm saying is that they can act. They might lack the sophistication, but they can act.

HE: I want to ask a very personal question.

SHE: Go ahead.

HE: Are you paid for all this?

SHE: Of course not.

HE: Then why do it?

SHE: Because, as I've said before, I wanted to help. I see injustice all around me. I feel guilty in my own small way. This is one aspect where I know I can assist.

HE: Will it make you sleep better at night?

SHE: Why do you keep fighting me? I don't think it relevant that I sleep better at night or not. If what I'm doing is wrong I won't do it. I'll stop. It's as easy as that. I'll stop. And I mean it. I want you with me tonight because I need someone who can tell me if I'm wrong. My methods might not be the best. I know there is something they resent. Whether in me or the play I don't know, but it's there. It's not something I can put my finger on. And I'm not giving up until I know what it is, and to what extent I am responsible. And I want you to help me to find out.

HE: Maybe you're relying too heavily on me. What qualifies a person like myself to sit in judgement over you, or anyone else for that matter?

SHE: Many things. Your experience with people both here and in England. You know what it is like there; you know what it is like here. I can never really know what it's like to be black ... from the inside. You must feel some resentment too.

HE: Towards you?

SHE: Yes, towards me.

HE: No, I don't think I feel resentment towards you. No, I don't think so. Let's smoke. I think I need a cigarette, even menthol.

Don't forget to stop at a shop, please.

SHE: Even a menthol?

fx: Match is struck

HE: You know, the power of advertising is such that people believe that menthol is a smokable cigarette.

SHE: You don't have to have it.

HE: Hobson's choice. Now, what do you propose to do this evening and what do you expect of me? Give me my instructions.

SHE: I'm not really sure. Play it by ear. Watch what happens, I suppose, and tell me afterwards. I can't imagine that they dislike the play; it's the type of thing they can do; the type of thing they can feel.

HE: You mean slavery?

SHE: Yes, as I've said, it's a part of their experience, a part out of their past. They can still feel it in the present. There is an identification.

HE: And this is being done at the whim of some foreigners?

SHE: I wouldn't put it like that. They asked me to put on something with the Nyanga Players, something original, and that's what I'm doing.

HE: And you think the Blacks will enjoy portraying their past? Or their present?

SHE: They might or might not enjoy it, but they can certainly do it . . . and with conviction.

HE: And your actors would want to do it . . . with conviction?

SHE: Yes, if you want to put it that way. But I know there is something wrong somewhere. I feel that certain things done by them are deliberate. They come late. They don't learn their lines. They seem surly.

HE: All of them?

SHE: Not all, but certainly the most talented.

HE: The most sensitive?

Long pause

SHE: I'm not sure what you are getting at.

HE: I'm getting at the fact that there might be some justification for their attitude. They might not like the image of the past, the portrayal of their humiliation, the reminder . . .

fx: Car screeches to a halt

HE: What's the matter? What was that in aid of?

SHE: Your shop, sir. Here I am sure, you can get cigarettes other than menthol.

fx: Car engine switched off
fx: Fade in car

SHE: [*slowly*] I don't suppose you can be expected to know exactly what the set up will be tonight, but from the little I have told you, does it seem as if I am in any way to blame? It worries me.

HE: I can't answer that. I can't pass judgement, since I don't know the facts. I am completely in the dark, and in terms of understanding attitudes I am more ignorant than you think. You asked me to come along because you thought that my advice could be relied upon. Correct? Shall I now make a confession?

SHE: If you wish to.

HE: I have very seldom been inside an African location and I have certainly never been inside Nyanga.

SHE: I can't believe it.

HE: Absolutely true. This is the first time I shall be going into a location since I was a child.

SHE: Have you no black friends?

HE: I knew one or two at university, but that is all. Do you realize that isolation in this country is by no means a white monopoly? We Browns are isolated from both Whites and Blacks. I've lived within a few miles of Nyanga most of my life, and yet I have never been there. But I have been to London, Rome and Paris. I've lived in the houses of Whites in Europe and never in the houses of Blacks here at home. For all I know I could still be living on Hampstead Heath.

SHE: You must be exaggerating. There is an African woman who cleans for you. Doesn't she come from Nyanga? Have you never been to her home?

HE: I have no idea whether she is African or otherwise. It never struck me as important to know. I suppose she must come from somewhere, but I have no idea whether Nyanga, Langa, Kensington, or whether she lives in someone's backyard in Constantia. I never really cared to find out since the occasion never really arose. She could come from a different world, a different planet.

SHE: And ...

HE: If she were not to turn up one day I wouldn't know where to start looking for her. I do this deliberately so as not to get involved with people. I dare not have too intimate friendships until I am abosolutely convinced. Of what I do not know. I can't

97

afford intimacies and involvements. I might seem selfish but I cannot afford to be hurt.

SHE: And this is how you live?

HE: This is how I live.

SHE: Could I be a friend of yours?

HE: I'm not sure.

SHE: *Am* I a friend of yours?

HE: I can't say. There are many factors.

SHE: Like colour?

HE: That is one of them. That could prove an obstacle, and then again it might not.

SHE: I'm beginning to wonder whether you really can help us tonight.

HE: Yes, I doubt I'll prove helpful. I don't really know why I came. Everything told me not to come. I could have told you this before, only I'm not sure I knew all this before. Why did I come and expose myself? Conscience? Morbid curiosity? To be of some help? Find a more objective view? No, none of these . . . or all of these. Maybe it is because you are . . . you. And the situation is . . . well, the situation is what it is. And I am me. I will most probably be even more confused after than I was before. I don't know. I really don't know.

SHE: What I want is for you to tell me whether I am wrong. I might very well be to blame. Although I feel that they don't resent me so much because I'm me, as the fact that they see me as a representative of the Whites.

HE: Then they would treat all Whites the same.

SHE: Well they do, don't they? I mean they might very well feel the same way but not be able to show it. In some cases they can, in other cases not. In my case they can. I am a woman. I'm defenceless. I have a conscience. And I'm trying to help.

HE: Maybe.

SHE: Then again their attitude might be a personal one. I was brought up in a hard school. My education was tough. When I did my drama training in Europe it was strict. If the Nyanga people want to be actors they must learn discipline. They cannot be late for performances and get away with it.

HE: Are you sure they really want to be actors?

SHE: In an amateur sort of way, yes. But they must learn to behave like actors. And no allowances because they are not professionals, or because they're Blacks.

HE: Or surly.

SHE: Or surly. Eight o'clock is eight o'clock in anybody's language. You wait and see. I guarantee they won't be on time. A few maybe, but the rest will stroll in at their leisure. I can give you quite a few examples. Would you accept that type of behaviour from anyone else?

HE: I don't know. The answer isn't a straightforward one. Allowances should be made for anyone, given the circumstances.

SHE: Well, haven't I made enough allowances already? How much more must I sacrifice because I'm white? Am I responsible for their oppression? Did I put them in locations? Must I suffer their unpunctuality in silence? Smile at their sneers? Enjoy their snide remarks in a language they know I can't understand? Must I suffer all this because I am prepared to give? To help? To assist?

HE: Careful now. Your acute martyrdom is showing.

SHE: And you also. You seem no different. You've been fighting me from the moment you got into the car. Whose side are you on? What more do you people want? Must I change my colour? Move to a location? Throw bombs? Do I deserve to be treated like this?

HE: Tell me, as a matter of interest, how *would* you like to be treated?

SHE: As a human being. A lady.

HE: Or a white lady?

fx: Peak car. Fade out
fx: Fade in car

HE: Possibly act four might prove to be the most interesting.

SHE: Act four? I'm not sure what you mean.

HE: Of your play. Act four of *Middle Passage*. You versus the Nyanga Players.

SHE: You think this will prove the most interesting?

HE: Or the most revealing, whichever you prefer.

SHE: Revealing of what?

HE: Well ... of attitudes. Human relationships. Of colour. Call it what you may. The best plays are always acted off stage. I know it's an unforgivable cliché but the best dramas are found in real life.

SHE: All the world's a stage and that sort of thing. Yes, you're right. I'm afraid it's a terrible cliché. It was said before ... better.

HE: How are we off for time? I'm developing a complex about being late. It's catching.

SHE: We'll be punctual, don't worry. There within a few minutes.

HE: This place is so new to me, the location I mean, it's like another planet, another world.

SHE: Nyanga? Yes, it does seem deserted doesn't it?

99

HE: I would have expected to find it crowded with people.

SHE: But there are people ...

HE: Yes, I know, there are people in the street. It is not unpeopled, it's deserted. There is a difference. Something important seems to be missing. Maybe it's the sameness. Something important seems to be missing. Maybe it's the sameness that gives one the illusion. The streets, the houses, the lights all seem the same. And there is something about the faces. They all seem to have the same expression, especially the adults. Almost a resigned look. Most probably it isn't so, but it seems so to me. Does it to you?

SHE: No. But then I know some of the people here.

HE: I have very few friends, and I don't choose them on grounds of colour.

SHE: But I know these people. I could invite them socially, to visit me in my flat, but I know they won't come.

HE: Have you tried?

SHE: No, I have not. But I just know they won't come. They'll say yes. They'll make promises. But in the end they won't turn up.

HE: Or if they had phones ... they'd take them off the hook.

fx: Long pause then car pulls to a halt. Car doors open

SHE: Here we are, dead on time.

fx: Car doors slammed shut

SHE: [*going off mic*] Will you follow me? This way.

fx: Pop music and voices are heard from behind a door

SHE: [*off mic*] This is it. We should have an interesting discusssion afterwards.

HE: [*coming on mic*] I wonder whether it will be necessary.

SHE: [*coming on mic*] This is the door to the hall. They're playing pop music.

fx: Door opens. Pop music very loud. Voices stop

SHE: [*whispering loudly close to mic above the music*] Please have a seat somewhere. See what I said? Five actors out of a cast of more than twenty. The rest might or might not turn up as the evening progresses. [*loudly moving slightly off mic*] Could we have that record off please!

fx: Music stops

Good evening everyone. Are we ready for work? As usual there are only a few of us. Let's hope the rest will turn up later. We can't afford to waste any time whatsoever. The show comes off in three weeks. So the sooner we begin tonight the better. We will just have to improvise as we go along. All right? Now then, let's start with the last act. Act three. We are now finally in the New World, on the plantations. Get into your positions. Could we have the new music on please?

fx: Missa Luba starts playing softly

SHE: Now then, all of you spread out more ... I want you to ... to make like slaves.

fx: Peak Missa Luba to end of a section

END

An Abandoned Bundle

Mbuyiseni Oswald Mtshali

> The morning mist
> and chimney smoke
> of White City Jabavu
> flowed thick yellow
> as pus oozing
> from a gigantic sore.
>
> It smothered our little houses
> like fish caught in a net.
>
> Scavenging dogs
> draped in red bandanas of blood
> fought fiercely
> for a squirming bundle.
>
> I threw a brick;
> they bared fangs
> flicked velvet tongues of scarlet
> and scurried away,
> leaving a mutilated corpse —
> an infant dumped on a rubbish heap —
> 'Oh! Baby in the Manger
> sleep well
> on human dung'.

Its mother
had melted into the rays of the rising sun,
her face glittering with innocence
her heart as pure as untrampled dew.

from Egoli

Matsemela Manaka

*The two men are sleeping again. They wake in a hurry. Hammy
rises first. John groans.*

HAMILTON: Are you dreaming?

JOHN: Yes. Chains, man, chains!

HAMILTON: Awu. And me too! [*They hear others getting up for work
and are galvanized into action, struggling into their workclothes,
boots, vests, helmets etc.*]

HAMILTON: Hey, tshayile wetu!

JOHN: Wait for me!

HAMILTON: Ezi zibanga zabelungu zizakuthi siphetwe yi babalaas!

*By now they are dressed and are adjusting their helmet lights but
not yet switching them on.*

JOHN: [*Greeting unseen workmates*] Haai, kunjani Ananias! Haai
sikhona!

*They are now coming to the front of the stage which is now lit as if
it were a mine shaft. As they move to it they turn on their helmet
lamps. The mine sequence is mimed with sound effects made by the
men. They make the drilling noises and work in harmony. Each
picks up a drill, carries it to his workplace, drills, pulls the drill
out. Kicks his spade into his hand using the back of the spade as a
lever, clears the hole for the dynamite stick. The placing of the stick
by the blaster is assumed, as the miners would not do that.*
*The two men crouch, with the spades at the side of their heads as
protection.*

JOHN: Tshisha! [*They block their noses, blow out their cheeks and
put their free hands over their unprotected ears.*]
There is an explosion.
*The two men casually get up and start preparing the pile of rubble
for the kibble which will soon descend; they call for it.*

JOHN: Caaable! [*He waits, pointing his lamp at the top of the shaft they are working in. After a moment he expresses his impatience.*] Msona mmao!
The cable descends as we gather from the way they wait for it. It supports a kibble about 8 foot high which they brace so that it sits firmly and without jolting on the ground. When it settles they start lashing, which is a rhythmic throwing upwards of the rubble, very fast, with the advantage that the backs of the spades, hitting the stage, set up a hell of a beat.
After a moment the kibbles are assumed to be full: don't be afraid of making the process a bit too long if it is well performed.

HAMILTON: [*Standing back and throwing up his light to the cable control*]: Caable! [*Pause*] Mnquntu! *The cable gets taken up and they prevent it from swinging.*
They go back to drilling, this time working face to face. They again go and wait for the blast, shielding themselves with their spades.

JOHN: Tshisha!

They wait for a similar pause to the previous one but instead of the normal explosion there is a larger one followed by what is clearly the roar of a collapsing shaft.
Lights blackout leaving only the headlamps. The men fall and grope about desperately.

JOHN: Hamilton! Put your headlamp on! Put your headlamp on!
HAMILTON: It's on!
JOHN: Zero 774116 over! Zero 774116 over!

Noise continues

HAMILTON: Where are you! Where are you!
JOHN: Over here! Come on! Move!
HAMILTON: Come on! Phone!
JOHN: I have been phoning! There is no answer.

Noise fades

HAMILTON: Keep on phoning!
JOHN: You try your luck then.

Hamilton tries but gets choked by dust and his own coughing.

HAMILTON: Take your thing.
JOHN: Hey, Hammy, look over there!

He points his headlamp across the stage.

HAMILTON: Where?

JOHN: There.

HAMILTON: Rats!

JOHN: Let's follow these rats.

HAMILTON: You take the lead.

They struggle across the stage. They give the impression that it is not at all even. There are piles and walls of rubble. Hamilton finally stands up, blocking John.

HAMILTON: Hey man, move!

JOHN: There are three ways here. Which do we take?

HAMILTON: Phone above.

JOHN: Zero 774116 over, Zero 774116 over.

There is a noise from his intercom.

JOHN: Yes sir, there are three ways here, which one do we take? Which one do we take? Over.

INTERCOM: *Long incomprehensible but aggressive jumble.*

HAMILTON: What does he say?

JOHN: He says we must decide.

HAMILTON: Decide!

JOHN: Hammy, there's a light over there.

HAMILTON: Where?

JOHN: There! Move your light. Over there. Let's go. Let's move!

They switch off their headlamps and loud music — Stimela — fills the theatre. Then it fades and the lights go up for next sequence. Back in the compound again. John is sitting on his box, drinking. Hammy has his head down. He is smoking, the room is a shambles, just as it was when they rushed to get up in the morning.

JOHN: Thanks God I was not in shaft seven. I would have collapsed with the earth. [*He is already quite drunk.*]

HAMILTON: Hey, musubhanxa wena. Other people died and you are busy thanking your God.

He stands up to go.

JOHN: Hey, Hammy, where are you getting to?

HAMILTON: To iBandla.

JOHN: Hey, man! The people of iBandla don't want to buy records. They don't even drink. What they know, it's mine politics.

HAMILTON: That's my taste. [*Exits*]

JOHN: Hammy's trying to be smart you know. He has forgotten all about where he comes from.

He turns on the radio — the real radio — probably on the English

Service but it could be anything — and listens disdainfully for a while and then makes an improvised comment on what he has heard — song or commentary. Then he turns on the music he really likes on his gram. MbaQanga. He dances to it drinking all the time. He sings and burps. He spills some beer down his bare chest and scoops it off his chest into his mouth. He then becomes quite ill. Staggers forward and finally vomits on the stage floor. He then collapses into his vomit.
Hammy enters, switches off the gram, comes and stands over the prostrate John.

HAMILTON: Hey, wetu. Somebody who shares the same surname with you died in Shaft Seven today.

JOHN: Haai, man. Stop interfering with my freedom.

HAMILTON: This is serious. His name is Oupa Ledwaba.

JOHN: Hammy, are you mad? Wahlanya wena! This world is too big and the people in it are too many. Even names can't cope up with their number. They share numbers and surnames.

HAMILTON: He could be your son.

JOHN: Not my son! Oupa, Oupa don't come. Oupa, stay at home, my son, Oupa, Oupa. [*He is collapsing in the vomit and the horror.*]

HAMILTON: [*Pulling him up and shaking him. Seeing it is useless, he drops him.*] I would not escape from prison to imprison myself in another poison like liquor. I pity the poor woman who gave birth to Oupa. Nobody must blame liquor. The blame goes to the man ablaze in it. [*He gets up and throws the letter he has brought in down on John.*]

JOHN: A letter for me? If it's for me, read it for me.

HAMILTON: [*Opens it and sits on his box to read it.*] 'Dear John...'

JOHN: Ya...[*As if answering*]

HAMILTON: 'I have lost my job. Baas Pienaar sold the farm to another baas. Children are starving because we had nothing to eat.' Poor souls!

JOHN: Hey, Hammy. I never said you should answer that letter. I only requested you to read it for me.

HAMILTON: She wants to know about the safety of her children.

JOHN: Safe from what?

HAMILTON: [*Pulling him to his feet and shaking him.*] According to this letter your children are eating soil and tree leaves. They are dying of hunger. They sleep with empty stomachs.

JOHN: No! Suzanne can't do that to me! She can't just let my children die without my consent!

105

HAMILTON: [*Moves forward as white mine official*] Waar is John Ledwaba? Waar is John Ledwaba?

JOHN: Hierso meneer.

HAMILTON: Come nearer.

JOHN: [*Struggling to stand*] Ja Meneer.

HAMILTON: Ja, jy's dronk, heh.

JOHN: Nie so dronk. Net 'n bietjie, Meneer.

HAMILTON: Tell me, do you know anybody by the name of Oupa Ledwaba?

JOHN: Ja, meneer, but I left my son at home.

HAMILTON: [*Under his breath*] Oo, Gods! [*Loud again*] We are very sorry, John. According to our records Oupa died in Shaft Seven. And you are free to go home any time from now. Verstaan jy? *Hamilton, at the back of the stage, has dropped the role of the official.*

JOHN: Then it is true.

HAMILTON: [*Turning on him*] True what?

JOHN: That he also passed away.

HAMILTON: I've been telling you! You kept on ignoring me!

JOHN: But how can he pass behind my eyes? I'm not blind. [*He coughs terribly*] I am also dying.

HAMILTON: I'm sorry John. The earth has done its job.

[*He takes John to his seat. Then, talking all the while, he goes to fetch water and a cloth to clean the vomit off the floor.*] But there is something very good about this earth. It does not discriminate. It swallows every colour that lives. It swallows every race. There is no racism about it. [*He changes the water and gets a clean cloth with which he wipes John's torso and face. The cleaning of the face is very gentle. Almost ceremonious.*] Your poor son is no more. Egoli has become the heart and the blood in every living soul. Now I'm afraid of death. [*He goes back to replace the water and cloth.*]

JOHN: [*Standing*] Oh God, how could you do that to my son? He might have become a liberator of Africa!

HAMILTON: Why look to heaven? Face the man! Nature knows why your son died, but we must not direct all our cries to God. Face the man! Your son will live with his ancestors. His spirit will not hang underneath the earth's crust but remain in our hearts. Don't let the death of your son kill your spirit. We all have the right to live. And we shall always sing a song with the calabash and spear next to our hearts.

JOHN: Let's give my son a spiritual burial. Never mind that his body is already buried three thousand feet underground. [*He points down.*]

They kneel together and mime the gathering of soil with their right hands. They raise it and let it flow through their fingers.

JOHN: Sweat turned into blood.

BOTH: Sweat turned into blood within the womb of Mother Africa.

JOHN: Infants turned into gold and diamonds.

BOTH: Infants turned into gold and diamonds in the presence of their parents.

JOHN: Sweat turned into blood.

They rise and place their hands on each other's shoulders.

BOTH: For justice, freedom and peace to prevail in the country of our forefathers, we shall all have to stand up and face the enemy without fear. We shall all have to worship the spear and drink blood from the calabash until we all sing the same song — *Uhuru* —

Azania
Uhuru
Azania

BLACKOUT

END

Notes

Egoli — Zulu for 'in Johannesburg, the City of Gold'

tshaylie wetu — Let's get going! It's knock-off time.

Ezi . . . babalaas! — These stupid whites will say we've got a hangover.

Haai . . . Sikhona! — Hey, how are you, Ananias! We're fine!

Tshisha — Watch out!

Msona mmao! — (Southern Sotho-derived slang): Backside (or genitals) of your mother

Mnquntu! — Zulu or Xhosa-derived: Penis (of animal);

musubhanxa wena — Don't fool around

MbaQanga, or *mbaqanga* — 'an African music mode which originated in Soweto, Johannesburg; according to purists, not jazz' (Branford Dictionary); popular township music

Hierso meneer — Afrikaans: Here, sir.

Ja, jy's dronk, heh — Afrikaans: Yes, you're drunk, hey.

Nie so . . . bietjie — Afrikaans: Not so drunk, just a bit.

Verstaan jy? — Afrikaans: Do you understand?

Uhuru — Swahili: freedom

Azania — term some black organizations have adopted for the future post-apartheid South Africa

Dust

Douglas Livingstone

The bundle in the gutter had its skull
cracked open by a kierie.
The blunt end of a sharpened bicycle
spoke grew a solitary
silver war-plume from the nape of his neck.
I turned him gently. He'd thinned to a wreck.

It was my friend Mketwa. He was dead.
Young Mac the Knife, I'd called him,
without much originality. Red
oozed where they'd overhauled him.
An illegal five-inch switchblade, his 'best'
possession, was stuck sideways in his chest.

He had been tough; moved gracefully, with ease.
We'd bricked, built walls, carted sand;
pitting strength against cement-bags, we'd seize
and humpf, steadied by a hand.
I paid the regulation wage plus fifty
per cent, his room, his board. He wasn't thrifty.

We were extending the old house I'd bought.
Those baked-lung middays we'd swill
the dust with cans of ice-cold beer. I thought
he must be unkillable,
except by white men. Each night the beerhall
took him: stoned wide, he would not stall or fall.

I don't think he learnt anything tangible
from me. From him, I learnt much:
his mother, cattle, kraal; the terrible
cheat that repaired his watch; such
and such pleased a woman; passes; bus queues;
whereabouts to buy stolen nails and screws.

His wife in Kwa Mashu, a concubine
in Chesterville, a mistress
in town: all pregnant. He'd bought turpentine
but they wouldn't drink it. This

was the trouble with women. Letters came
we couldn't read. He found another dame.

He left — more money, walls half-done, him tight —
to join Ital-Constructions.
Perhaps it had been white men: I am white.
Now, I phoned the ambulance
and sat with him. It came for Mac the Knife;
bore his corpse away; not out of my life.

Notes
kraal — Afrikaans: homestead, clan, community

To Lucky with his Guitar on a Grahamstown Street

Chris Zithulele Mann

Here comes Lucky, the tallest of the tall;
born in P E; raised on a farm; not young
(nineteen); hardly been to school (no money);
can't find a job (no schooling); clouds of
brisk-eyed sparrows perch inside his guitar.

So here's Lucky, Coolhand Lucky the Tall;
Sunday afternoon; easing into town;
hasn't a word (drifting over New Street);
nothing to tell us (tapping the pavement);
but Coolhand riffs; zig-zag bass; stringshine chords.

And here's a car; a Chevvy; it's slowing,
it's parking. Nope. The missus is waving.
She's scared. Nope, she's angry; she has something
to say, yes, she's rolling down the window.
Lady? 'What are you kaffirs doing in town?'

Silence; the tar's wet; a truck bakes and ticks.
For Christ's sake, say something! You're the tallest,
Lucky, give it to her! Stupid old bitch.
Here it comes ... Nope. Coolhand won't stop riffing.
The notes fly up like sparrows (for today).

African Trombone

Xolile Guma

It was a clear October morning, graced by the warmth of the sun, caressed by a capricious breeze typical of such a morning in sub-equatorial Africa. Towards the arena they came, in all shapes and sizes. Big ones, small ones, tall ones, short ones, fat ones, thin ones, a seething mass of people. Colourfully adorned in costumes of origin as varied as the people who wore them. Africans, independent Africans, proud of their independence and gathered now to celebrate the occasion, commemorating the day on which the colonial flag was brought down and theirs slowly and triumphantly raised to the heavens, there to flutter and sway, symbol of the African dream accomplished; Africans — and known as such, not the 'native hordes' of the old textbook descriptions, descending onto the plains to meet the long-haired gentlemen from across the sea.

Within the arena, festivities had begun. The army, resplendent in their new uniforms, stood in formation in the centre, flanked on the left by the youth league, on the right by the police, while in the background one saw 'Dad's army', veterans of the Second World War. How graphically that arena portrayed history, the old and the new, unable to merge but seemingly capable of peaceful co-existence. The neat, disciplined, modern, rectangular formation of the armed forces framed by the veterans: rugged, too old for discipline, out-dated, standing in a rough semi-circle, a formation dating back to the Africa which was being rediscovered.

I sat in the covered area immediately to the left of the seats reserved for 'honourable members of the diplomatic corps'. Further to the left, people were streaming in through all possible gates, filling whatever space there was, losing themselves in that sea of people with amazing ease. To the right, beyond a stately row of red seats enclosed by a green rope threaded through a progression of stainless steel rings, the sea of faces flowed endlessly, reaching the furthest boundaries of the arena, finally merging into the people to my left, thus completing the circle, punctuated only by the red hiatus, reserved for foreign emissaries and 'honourable members of the diplomatic corps'.

Intent as I was on surveying the panorama bedecking that green arena, my attention was arrested by one piercing note. The semi-circle composed of the veterans was now alive with motion, swaying

110

in a manner not unlike a giant millepede unsuccessfully attempting to do the twist: unco-ordinated and ragged and yet, in some grotesque way, orderly. Nor did the matter end there, for from that undisciplined writhing mass came sounds, rich sounds of deep voices, tremulously raised in haphazard fashion, accompanied by the honking of an assortment of brassware; bugles, trumpets, French horns, all relics of the Second World War, manfully handled by the veterans. And then I saw him, resplendent in the uniform of a regimental sergeant-major, medals proudly displayed, complemented by a loin-cloth of cowhide, feet encased in brown boots which had long resigned themselves to the inevitability of decay, blowing a trombone. He emerged from the ranks, taking halting, measured steps, veins bulging from the neck upwards, testimony of the magnitude of his exertion, blowing his trombone. Bent double but refusing to be cowed, his face lined by years of insecurity and anguish, hands gnarled by the experience of war and the passage of time, he blew his trombone. His trombone became vehicle of his emotions, emotions aroused by his peers, who like himself had actively fought for the day when their country would be free. The notes emanating from that trombone were not amenable to chromatic definition: they emanated from his guts and seemed to be directed at my guts, like the sound of a cow being slaughtered, blood flowing in viscous rivulets of red, drawing my stomach along for companionship. 'What does all this mean?' he seemed to be saying. 'Is this what I fought for, all those many years ago?' I watched transfixed. I could imagine the scene as it must have been thirty years earlier, in this same arena, when the then young men answered the call to arms. How straight and tall they must have stood then. Fired by the zeal of youth, prepared to die for their country. Now they were bent double.

The British ambassador's daughter, seated in the red hiatus, lisped 'Goth, ithn't that old man wif the trombone thweet?'

Intent on discovering the truth about that old man, I made my way through the crowds, pushing and heaving, cursing and pleading as the occasion demanded, until I too emerged through the iron gate leading out of the arena, feeling as I did so, as exalted as I would imagine the biblical camel feels when it manages to negotiate the proverbial eye of the needle. My task seemed almost hopeless. Where amongst that impossible mob, was I going to find an aged man, member of a royal regiment, in the uniform of a regimental sergeant-major, carrying a shiny trombone, whom the British ambassador's daughter had described as 'thweet'? On every side the people thronged, ululating and gesticulating in wild abandon,

111

emerging from that arena as though it was a giant dam, pregnant with people, whose sluice gates had just been opened. I reluctantly decided to drown myself in that sea of people, to be carried along by it like some bottle tossed in desperation by a marooned sailor, he not knowing where it would land, but hopeful that it would.

I 'landed' in town, part of a band of travellers which had boarded a bus whose bonnet bore some resemblance to a pig's snout. Looking about me, I noticed that people were gravitating towards various centres of amusement: pubs and discotheques, with neon lights brazenly announcing their wares. The bus stop was opposite a church whose wares, not being amenable to advertisement by neon lights, were surreptitiously implicit in the mystical darkness which it exuded. I paused a while, reflecting on all that had passed. The green snout coughed as the bus, 'Maphala Special: Never Say Die', jerked into clumsy motion, panting blue smoke through its posterior; low and squat, straddling the road like an overfed pig, obviously intent on returning to the arena, there to swallow more people before returning once again to relieve itself before the church.

The sun setting in the western sky spread the last rays of day with the tenderness of a mother laying her first-born to sleep. In the east, the moon made its coy appearance. Depressed by my inability to locate the trombonist, and yet soothed by the sky's version of the day's aftermath, I stood, pensive.

A woman came walking down the street towards me, with the strange, jerky gait peculiar to one who is two-in-one. I say a woman, in fact she was more of a girl than a woman, with narrow shoulders accentuating the bulge which was the source of her discomfort. As she passed, she seemed to smile ever so slightly, obviously amused by what must have been a look of incredulity on my face. 'Men,' she seemed to be saying, 'can never understand these things. Theirs is only to plant the seed — forgetting that, given a fertile environment, that seed must prosper and grow.' She waddled on, pausing to examine the flow of traffic before crossing to the church, eternal refuge of the desperate. To this day, I still wonder which startled me more, the sound of that piercing trombone, or the frenzied sceech of tyres. I jumped, startled, rudely jolted by the reality of life and death. She lay in a pool of blood, which only seconds earlier had given radiance to her coy smile; blood which only seconds earlier had held the promise of life. He came prancing down the street, rejuvenated by heaven-knows-what, trombone in hand. Absent was any of the 'thweetness' which the British ambassador's daughter might have seen. This was a man driven by frustration, like a lion mortally wounded, maddened by pain and seeking revenge. Cognizant of the fact that death was at hand, and yet mindful of the sweetness of life, he pranced down the street, coming towards us.

Meanwhile the crowds had converged on that pitiful spectacle; drawn and yet repelled by the horror of it. Like green flies around a dump of manure they buzzed, none venturing to do anything and none prepared to sacrifice his vantage point. 'Get the police somebody,' I howled, and immediately felt ashamed. Why the hell wouldn't I go and fetch the police? The refrain was picked up by others. 'Get the police, somebody!' — and still she bled.

The cavernous door of the church opened and the priest emerged. We all breathed a sigh of relief. The minister was come, defender of the faith, anointer of God, healer supreme; for who, but the minister, can heal what he cannot see? His appearance was greeted by a frenzied run of notes from the trombonist. Like an angel in mourning, white upon black, the minister floated out of the church.

'Do not touch that woman, old one,' he said, 'she needs medical attention which you are not capable of giving.'

Frightened by the tone of the 'angel', the old man who had been cradling the injured woman, let go. Her head hit the ground with a sickening thud; we all winced simultaneously.

'Fool,' the angel roared, 'now look what you've done.'

The old man picked up his trombone from the congealing blood, shook his head slowly from side to side, and began to walk away.

'Do you know who I am, young man?' he whispered, obviously hurt. I edged a little closer, hopefully.

'Be gone old one,' the minister threatened, 'your filthy loin skin and unwashed hands have already done damage not only to this poor woman but to us all. We who have self-respect and acceptable standards of conduct.'

He left, trombone in hand, disappearing into the night. To this day I have not been able to find him, possessor of the history of this land, without whose efforts we would not today be where we are. What he said to me with that trombone was, 'What is this independence for which I fought, but which now passes me by? Children for whom I selected education and not bribery as a means of salvation now use that education as a means of bribery, and call me a fool. I must stand as a curio for children. But always remember that with my death, your greatest source of information also dies. You will become the curiosity of the international society, a people denying their history.'

If you ever meet an old man carrying a trombone, or as is more likely, blowing his trombone, stop and listen. That African trombone has a great deal to say, and not much time in which to say it.

Sitting on the Balcony

Charles Mungoshi

Sitting on the balcony
fingering a glass of beer
I have bought without
any intention to drink —
I see a little boy
poking for something
in a refuse dump—
looking for a future?
I am afraid, the stars say
your road leads to another
balcony just like this one
where you will sit fingering
a beer you have bought without
any intention to drink.

Important Matters

Charles Mungoshi

There are important matters on the agenda —
matters of life and death.
The gravity and importance of these matters
showed in our deeply furrowed faces
as we sat watching the empty throne
waiting for the chairman who was already hours late
to come and open the meeting
although each of us secretly felt and wished
he would come in and just say.
Call it a day, boys!

Hours later, a messenger came in to say
the chairman had taken his girl
for a boatride on Lake McIlwaine.

We sat hunched round the empty chair —
the day suddenly pulled from right under us.

There and then we began to plan an air-tight plot
that would without fail bring about the downfall
of the chairman.
We looked at the plan from all angles
under all kinds of light
and when we were satisfied with it
we stepped out into the evening world
clutching our bags with faces that said
It's been a trying day.

Points for discussion

• There are several ways of building atmosphere. In this section you see
one technique at work in three different pieces (the la Guma, the Rive
short story and the Pillay): the writer selects, sifts, narrows down to
those sights, sounds, smells, human types, activities that will all add up to
the atmosphere-mosaic he wants.

• In this opening extract from A WALK IN THE NIGHT, after his
encounter with the policemen, is it obvious to you how Michael Adonis is
going to end his evening?

• Look at the way Richard Rive has built the character of Solly in RAIN.
If you make an 'inventory' of his physical and apparent social attributes, he
appears to be a thoroughly unpleasant and unfriendly personality. Yet — is
that really so?

• PARADISE is a poem written after District Six had had all the life,
spirit and character bulldozed out of it by government decree. It's a sad,
nostalgic poem, but how does the poet create this sadness? He doesn't in
any way paint a picture of the aliveness of the place in its heyday (as la
Guma and Rive did): what does he do instead? What do you think of the
last two lines?

• Notice the shaping of Dan Pillay's HOME, and the way in which
something as obvious as paragraphing helps to guide the reader through
the piece. And, of course, how else to end it but with the reappearance of
Seela! (Incidentally, this piece was written while the writer was still at
school, aged seventeen.)

• Do you enjoy Fhazel Johennesse's understated final stanza in LIVING IN
A FLAT IN ELDORADO PARK? Do you detect an element of irony here?

• MAKE LIKE SLAVES is the kind of piece that makes you want to
cringe. SHE's a real embarrassment, isn't she? The kind of person who,
some years ago, gave white liberals a bad name! Does her type still exist?
And — think carefully about this — does Rive blame *her* for everything, or
is HE a bit of a pain too?

• AN ABANDONED BUNDLE is extraordinary for several reasons. Let's look at the images first. Can you say that the image of the morning smoke as pus oozing from a sore works? Are the two elements of the image linked well-enough by some common ground? Does the fish/net houses/smoke image in stanza two work? And what about the near-lurid red-scarlet images that follow? But, perhaps more important than any of these things, what do you gather to be the author's attitude towards the mother as expressed in the last stanza? Is he being sharply critical of her or is there no irony in the 'innocence' and 'pure as untrampled dew'? Where would you place the blame for the horrific violence depicted here?

• Much of current black theatre in South Africa is very — and wonderfully — dependent on the physical impersonation and improvisation of the actors. From Manaka's published text, can you get an idea of the way he wants the actors to play EGOLI? From what you have read, what would the actors contribute which the published text can only suggest?

• Here, in DUST, is a white man offering some sort of help to a black man: but he's totally different from SHE in MAKE LIKE SLAVES, isn't he? In what ways? What are the implied comments about Mketwa's life as a city-man? Would he fit easily — or at all — into the rural family kraal/homestead?

• Lucky in Chris Zithulèle Mann's poem is very different: a real city-slicker. What do you think of him? Do you approve of his style, his way of doing things, his treatment of the 'missus' in her car? What would you have said to her? Then try it the other way around: be her, and decide what you would have said to Lucky and his friends when you rolled down the window.

• Xolile Guma gives an insight into immediately-post-Independence Southern Africa that is unnerving. Who is to blame? With whom do you sympathise? How is one ever going to give rightful place and position to all these different and disparate influences in what now makes up modern Southern Africa?

• The two Mungoshi poems that end this section are both pretty cynical observations by a person disillusioned with the achievements of independence. Especially as the poet lives in Zimbabwe, one is tempted to ask: Is it really as awful, as dispiriting, as Mungoshi makes out? Or is his selectivity giving only a partial — and therefore unfair — picture?

On the trains

For hundreds of thousands of South Africans each working day starts with the journey by train from a township or location or housing estate to the city; and it is often late evening before the return journey is made. In his poem, *City Johannesburg* Mongane Serote says:

> I travel ...
> Through your thick iron breath that you inhale
> At six in the morning and exhale from five noon.

So the trains and the things that happen on them form a relatively large chunk of experience for many South Africans. It is my guess that virtually no white South Africans know anything at all, at firsthand, about the things described in the following pieces:

The Dube Train

Can Themba

The morning was too cold for a summer morning, at least, to me, a child of the sun. But then on all Monday mornings I feel rotten and shivering, with a clogged feeling in the chest and a nauseous churning in the stomach. It debilitates my interest in the whole world around me.

The Dube Station with the prospect of congested trains, filled with sour-smelling humanity, did not improve my impression of a hostile life directing its malevolence plumb at me. All sorts of disgruntledties darted through my brain: the lateness of the trains, the shoving savagery of the crowds, the grey aspect around me. Even the announcer over the loudspeaker gave confused directions. I suppose it had something to do with the peculiar chemistry of the

117

body on Monday morning. But for me all was wrong with the world.

Yet, by one of those flukes that occur in all routines, the train I caught was not full when it came. I usually try to avoid seats next to the door, but sometimes it cannot be helped. So it was that Monday morning when I hopped into the Third Class carriage. As the train moved off, I leaned out of the paneless window and looked lacklustrely at the leaden platform churning away beneath me like a fast conveyer belt.

Two or three yards away, a door had been broken and repaired with masonite so that it would be an opening door no more. Moreover, just there a seat was missing, and there was a kind of a hall.

I was sitting opposite a hulk of a man; his hugeness was obtrusive to the sight when you saw him, and to the mind when you looked away. His head tilted to one side in a half-drowsy position, with flaring nostrils and trembling lips. He looked like a kind of genie, pretending to sleep but watching your every nefarious intention. His chin was stubbled with crisp, little black barbs. The neck was thick and corded, and the enormous chest was a live barrel that heaved forth and back. The overall he wore was open almost down to the navel, and he seemed to have nothing else underneath. I stared, fascinated, at his large breasts with their winking, dark nipples.

With the rocking of the train as it rolled towards Phefeni Station, he swayed slightly this way and that, and now and then he lazily chanted a township ditty. The titillating bawdiness of the words incited no humour or lechery or significance. The words were words, the tune was just a tune.

Above and around him, the other passengers, looking Monday-bleared, had no enthusiasm about them. They were just like the lights of the carriage — dull, dreary, undramatic. Almost as if they, too, felt that they should not be alight during the day.

Phefeni Station rushed at us with human faces blurring past. When the train stopped, in stepped a girl. She must have been a mere child. Not just *petite*, but juvenile in structure. Yet her manner was all adult as if she knew all about 'this sorry scheme of things entire' and with a scornful toss relegated it. She had the premature features of the township girls, pert, arrogant, live. There was that air about her that petrified any grown-ups who might think of asking for her seat. She sat next to me.

The train slid into Phomolong. Against the red-brick waiting-room I saw a *tsotsi* lounging, for all the world not a damn interested in taking the train, but I knew the type, so I watched him in grim anticipation. When the train started sailing out of the platform, he turned round nonchalantly and tripped along backwards towards an open door. It amazes me no end how these boys know exactly where the edge of the platform comes when they run like that backwards. Just at the drop he caught the ledge of the train and heaved himself in gracefully.

He swaggered towards us and stood between our seats with his back to the outside, his arms gripping the frame of the paneless window. He noticed the girl and started teasing her. All township love-making is rough.

'*Hi*, rubberneck!' — he clutched at her pear-like breast jutting from her sweater — 'how long did you think you'll duck me?'

She looked round in panic; at me, at the old lady opposite her, at the hulk of a man opposite me. Then she whimpered, 'Ah, *Au-boetie*, I don't even know you.'

The *tsotsi* snarled, 'You don't know me, eh? You don't know me when you're sitting with your student friends. You don't know last night, too, *nê*? You don't know how you ducked me?'

Some woman, reasonably out of reach, murmured, 'The children of today . . .' in a drifting sort of way.

Mzimhlophe, the dirty-white station.

The *tsotsi* turned round and looked out of the window on to the platform. He recognized some of his friends there and hailed them.

'O, Zigzagza, it's how there?'

'It's jewish!'

'*Hela*, Tholo, my ma hears me, I want that ten-'n-six!'

'Go get it in hell!'

'Weh, my sister, don't lissen to that guy. Tell him Shakespeare nev'r said so!'

The gibberish exchange was all in exuberant superlatives.

The train left the platform in the echoes of its stridency. A washer-women had just got shoved into it by ungallant males, bundle and all. People in the train made sympathetic noises, but too many passengers had seen too many tragedies to be rattled by this incident. They just remained bleared.

As the train approached New Canada, the confluence of the Orlando and the Dube train lines, I looked over the head of the girl next to me. It must have been a crazy engineer who had designed this crossing. The Orlando train comes from the right. It crosses the Dube train overhead just before we reach New Canada. But when it reaches the station it is on the right again, for the Johannesburg train enters extreme left. It is a curious kind of game.

Moreover, it has necessitated cutting the hill and building a bridge. But just this quirk of an engineer's imagination has left a spectacularly beautiful scene. After the drab, chocolate-box houses of the township, monotonously identical row upon row, this gash of man's imposition upon nature never fails to intrigue me.

Our caveman lover was still at the girl while people were changing from our train to the Westgate train in New Canada. The girl wanted to get off, but the *tsotsi* would not let her. When the train left the station, he gave her a vicious slap across the face so that her beret went flying. She flung a leg over me and rolled across my lap in her hurtling escape. The *tsotsi* followed, and as he passed me he reeled with the sway of the train.

To steady himself, he put a full paw in my face. It smelled sweaty-sour. Then he ploughed through the humanity of the train, after the girl. Men gave way shamelessly, but one woman would not take it. She burst into a spitfire tirade that whiplashed at the men.

'Lord, you call yourself men, you poltroons! You let a small ruffian insult you. Fancy, he grabs at a girl in front of you — might be your daughter — this thing with the manner of a pig! If there were real men here, they'd pull his pants off and give him such a leathering he'd never sit down for a week. But, no, you let him do this here; tonight you'll let him do it in your homes. And all you do is whimper, "The children of today have never no respect!" *Sies!'*

The men winced. They said nothing, merely looked around at each other in shy embarrassment. But those barbed words had brought the little thug to a stop. He turned round, scowled at the woman, and with cold calculation cursed her anatomically, twisting his lips to give the word the full measure of its horror.

It was like the son of Ham finding a word for his awful discovery. It was like an impression that shuddered the throne of God Almighty. It was both a defilement and a defiance.

'Hela, you street-urchin, that woman is your mother,' came the shrill voice of the big hulk of a man, who had all the time sat quietly opposite me, humming his lewd little township ditty. Now he moved towards where the *tsotsi* stood rooted.

There was menace in every swing of his clumsy movements, and the half-mumbled tune of his song sounded like under-breath cursing for all its calmness. The carriage froze into silence.

Suddenly, the woman shrieked and men scampered on to seats. The *tsotsi* had drawn a sheath-knife, and he faced the big man.

There is something odd that a knife does to various people in a crowd. Most women go into pointless clamour, sometimes even hugging round the arms the men who might fight for them. Some men make gangway, stampeding helter-skelter; but with that hulk of man the sight of the gleaming blade in the *tsotsi*'s hand, drove him beserk. The splashing people left a sort of arena. There was an evil leer in his eye, much as if he was experiencing satanic satisfaction.

Croesus Cemetery flashed past.

Seconds before the impact, the *tsotsi* lifted the blade and plunged it obliquely. Like an instinctual, predatory beast, he seemed to know exactly where the vulnerable jugular was and he aimed for it. The jerk of the train deflected his stroke, though, and the blade slit a long cleavage down the big man's open chest.

With a demoniacal scream, the big man reached out for the boy crudely, careless now of the blade that made another gash in his arm. He caught the boy by the upper arm with the left hand, and between the legs with the right and lifted him bodily. Then he hurled him towards me. The flight went clean through the paneless window, and only a long cry trailed in the wake of the rushing train.

It was so sudden that the passengers were galvanized into action, darting to the windows; the human missile was nowhere to be seen. It was not a fight proper, not a full-blown quarrel. It was just an incident in the morning Dube train.

The big man, bespattered with blood, got off at Langlaagte Station. Only after we had left the station did the stunned passengers break out into a cacophony of chattering.

Odd, that no one expressed sympathy for the boy or man. They were just greedily relishing the thrilling episode of the morning.

Notes

tsotsi — 'a usually flashily dressed African street thug, frequently a member of a gang, armed with a knife on other weapon' (Branford Dictionary). It's origin is unclear: it could be a corruption of 'zoot-suit'; or derived from the verb 'tsotsile' = dressed in narrow trousers; or derived just from acharacteristic whistle. The street-language of the townships is called 'tsotsi-taal', 'taal' being the Africans for 'language'

jewish — fine, first-class, usually referring to expensive clothes

boetie — Afrikaans: brother

Mzimphlophe, the dirty white station — a pun: '-mhlophe' means 'white'

Sies! — expression of disgust

Dube Train Revisited

Mbulelo Mzamane

For Gangi and Can

The third-class carriage was almost deserted as Gangi and I boarded the train at Dube. One or two people were gazing, expressionless, through the window; others wore blank stares focused at no point in particular. It was almost midday and the midsummer sun was oven-hot.

At Phefeni a woman with a child strapped to her back came in. She grabbed my shoulders for support as the train jerked off.

'*Dankie, my kind,*' she said as soon as she'd regained her balance and edged, tortoise-like, towards the nearest vacant seat.

I dozed off and only opened my eyes slightly at Phomolong. However, Mzimhlophe promised excitement and so I kept awake. Wonder Boy's gang was at the station. Wonder Boy was the champion 'staffrider' of Soweto. He could drop off the first coach of a moving train and run backwards to catch the last coach called *dumani*. He had several apprentices most of whom we found hanging around Mzimhlophe. When the train pulled off, I craned my neck so as to miss very little. They still stood nonchalantly, leaning against the toilets and passing a *stompie* round. Before the *dumani* had pulled away from the platform they were all in the train.

I was falling asleep again when the train made another jolting halt at New Canada junction. A few passengers got off to change trains, others came in. The train moved off, with another performance by Wonder Boy's gang who, however, remained at New Canada waiting for a train back to the township.

'Why should people gamble with their lives like so?' the old lady with the child asked.

A general discussion followed on the suicidal tendencies of township youth.

Before we reached Croesus the end doors of our coach burst open, almost simultaneously. A group of boys carrying packets of sweets came in.

Something odd happened. From one end of the coach one of the boys with a greasy Dobbs hat on, started distributing sweets to every passenger, without demanding any payment. '*Dankie, my kind,*' the fat lady with the child said.

122

I looked at Gangi but he was asleep.

There were about ten of them, each wearing a single earring, Champion Jack Dupree style. On their heads an assortment of hats sat precariously perched and pulled to within a negligible distance of their eyes. They wore mucky khaki pants and greasy dustcoats that made them look like faithful garage attendants. They had on off-white P.F. tennis shoes.

From my knowledge of the type I knew there was trouble brewing. The rough manner in which the packet of jube-jubes was thrust into my folded arms confirmed my suspicions. I was still wondering what they were celebrating when, after walking the length of the coach, Greasy Dobbs took off his hat and, holding it like a collector's dish in church, waved it at the last recipient of his sweets, who unquestioningly dipped his hands in his pockets and obligingly deposited his contribution.

The rest of the gang had spread themselves at strategic points, mainly around the exits, all along the coach. One or two were playing conspicuously with scotch knives and 'three stars', hurling them into the air and catching them most dexterously. Their facial expressions reminded me of Richard Widmark in the movies, after a successful operation.

As Greasy Dobbs drew nearer panic seized me. I remembered I'd no money.

After waking Gangi up with a slight kick, I signalled to him by rubbing my thumb against index finger. He didn't seem to understand. I spoke the word in a whisper.

'What for?' he shouted.

I could have strangled him, only I hate scenes.

Gangi's eyes dropped to the packet of malted toffees on his lap. He saw that I also had sweets.

'But I don't want these.' He was speaking more softly.

'You'll have to pay for them, same as everybody in this coach,' I said. 'Let me have some money.'

He stealthily put his hand in his pocket and brought out a twenty-cent piece, which I quickly snatched.

Out of the corner of my eye I saw his hand to return his pocket but Greasy Dobbs was already upon us. He thrust his filthy hat in my direction. I responded accordingly. Twenty cents for a packet of jube-jubes worth only five cents!

The train stopped at Mayfair. The group got off the train and made the V-sign at us.

At Braamfontein we all got off. It suddenly occurred to me that none of the passengers in our coach had got off between New

Canada and Braamfontein. I thought it funny that everybody going to Braamfontein should have gathered in the same coach.

'Sies!' the fat lady with the child said. 'My ten cents gone for a worthless packet of sweets which even my grandchild here refuses to touch.'

We walked towards the platform attendants in silence until a well-dressed, wealthy-looking man with a tubby tummy spoke.

'I'd no change so I gave them a rand,' he said.

The fat lady adjusted the child on her back and then flung the packet of mints onto the rails.

'What explanation am I to give to the guards? *Ke tla reng*? My ticket ends at Croesus and here I am, four stations away. Where am I going to get the money from? She spat in front of the man who looked like a tycoon and then continued. 'You'd imagine there were no men with us. *Ke banna lintho tsee*? Those who'd stand by and watch their wives and daughters being raped by uncircumcised baboons?'

Gangi and I increased our pace.

We were among the lucky ones because our tickets ended at Park Station, a station further, where we'd arranged to meet our girlfriends and take them to the movies. But no matter. We could walk to Park Station.

'*Uyasinyela lomfazi*,' Gangi said. 'Did she expect us to pull a James Bond on those chaps, unarmed? She can take her case to the police if she wants to.'

'*Ja*, we'd have been cut to pieces,' I said.

'I'll explain to Thembi.' Thembi was his girlfriend. 'We can't go to the movies. I've used up all the money. Bloody *kalkoens*! *Abomangca bamasimba*, *net*! A whole five rand!'

I was speechless.

We walked to Park Station. Frankly, my heart was no longer in it. I didn't care to explain anything to anybody, least of all to my girlfriend.

At Park Station I was greatly relieved to find that our girlfriends were nowhere in sight. We were more than an hour late.

'Maybe they gave us up,' I said.

Gangi agreed and we made no attempt to look for them.

We weren't in a hurry to go home. If only we could loiter around the station for the next two hours, we could travel back in a group. The boys — I had in mind the more muscular of our friends like Phambili, Scara and S'divane — would knock off at five. We'd waylay them so that we would have the protection of their company in the train.

We decided to hang around 'Parky'. But we didn't remain there for long.

A police van turned the corner.

I felt the police had entered into a conspiracy with the train robbers. I'd seen them on several occasions stopping people for passes around the station in the morning, but never in the afternoon.

'*Ndoda kuyanyiwa la, asambe,*' I told Gangi, and so we went off in the direction of town where comparative safety lay.

At five the police were still there, and so we missed the boys.

Our people have a saying that those who've once met will meet again. As Gangi and I pushed our way into the overcrowded train amidst cries of, '*Fuduwa ousi, mothule ka libono*' I spotted Greasy Dobbs. I wanted to bolt, but the people pushed me from behind until I was standing with my well-trimmed moustache almost touching this fellow's soiled dustcoat. A few yards away Gangi was grinning, obviously unaware of the impending disaster. There was just no way I could communicate with him.

As the train pulled off Greasy Dobbs threw me an intimidating stare. I immediately dropped my eyes.

He started working his fingers into some old man's pockets, took out what looked like a purse and put it in his pocket.

As he worked his way away from me, I sighed so loudly that the old man who had just been searched looked back at me. Our eyes met but I immediately lowered mine.

Genuine relief simply refused to come my way. A hollow feeling lingered in my chest. Why should I not tell this old man he'd been searched? Probably his whole pay packet. Those eyes troubled me. It could have been my father. If I exposed Greasy Dobbs the whole train would probably pounce upon him. But what if they watched him carve me? You're bloody yellow, a different voice kept harping. Greasy Dobbs is better. At least, he has the courage of his evil convictions.

I began sweating like an athlete. Frankly, I would have been happier running the twelve miles home than travelling in that cursed train.

We got off at Dube and followed the human stream out of the platform, like logs in a flood.

'Gangi,' I said 'did you see that chap . . .'

Madoda! Before I'd finished the sentence I saw Greasy Dobbs and three of his decoys immediately behind us. Fortunately they didn't seem to recognize us.

'Which chap?' Gangi asked.

I pulled him by the elbow and placed one finger on my mouth.

As they passed by Greasy Dobbs dropped an object which looked rather familiar to me. Gangi, too, noticed and made as if to tell them.

'Have you no sense, man?' I whispered. 'Can't you see who those chaps are?'

He violently pulled my arm and we turned back. People started cursing at us as we bumped into them, but we had to get back.

We waited for the people to clear. Not until we were absolutely certain Greasy Dobbs and his gang had left did we go and see what object he had dropped. It lay where he'd dropped it. It was a pass. I opened it and looked at the photo. Familiar eyes stared at me.

'*Uyamazi*?' Gangi asked.

'Yes, I saw him in the train,' I said. 'Greasy Dobbs was searching him right in front of my eyes.'

'Was there no way of alerting him?'

I seldom entertain silly questions.

Notes

Dankie, my kind — Afrikaans: Thank you, my child

Staffrider — see commentary-link before the poem STAFFRIDER on page 139

Ke tla reng — What shall I say?

Ke banna lintho tsee — Southern Sotho: These things are men (literally: they're men these things)

Uyasinyela lomfazi — This woman is talking shit

kalkoen — Afrikaans: turkey

Abomangca bamasimba — They are shit

'Noda kuyanyiwa la, asambe — Man, it's tough here, let's go

Fuduwa . . . — Come, old sister, move your buttocks

Madoda — familiar address, abbreviation of 'amadoda', men

Uyamazi — Do you know him?

The Night Train

Fhazel Johennesse

there is no comfort here
in this third class coach
on this green resisting seat
i twitch and glance around —
there are few too few travellers
on the night train
crossing my legs and flicking

my cigarette I turn to stare
through the window
into the darkness outside
(or is it my reflection I stare at)
and glance impatiently at the wrong
stations we stop at
out
i must get out of here soon
for in this coach there is a smell
which haunts me
not the smell of stale man but
the whispering nagging smell of fear

Bye Bye, Overcoat

Mutiswayo Shandu

The day before yesterday Mr Straun
gives me this overcoat. Today I catch
this train to my Stepmother's, wearing it.
It is a splendid coat, fawn, almost new
— just this small gap in the seam of one sleeve.

It is past midday, the train not crowded
with mostly shoppers and halfday meisies.
Still, I am standing, straphanging, swaying
but I prefer it: such a cool garment
of such swaggering cut should not be creased.

Comes payday: a good hat — maybe a fine
snapbrim fedora, perhaps from PATEL'S
is quite definitely indicated.
Stepmama has a Singer at her place ...
The air around me goes into deepfreeze.

Turning, I see at the far end: Main Ou
has joined us, accompanied by a pair
of toughlooking tsotsis. Over dozens
of heads his eyes meet mine. He is staring
at my new overcoat. Tixo! Such luck!

127

They start working the silent, sullen folks,
towards me: peering in wallets, purses,
emptying handbags; some men have to stand
to have their back-pockets patted. Main Ou
does not work or hang on. His legs are braced.

He hardly moves with the train's rock and roll.
He taps a bicyclespoke with a stained
wood handle, coolly, on his left thumbnail.
His two thugs work quietly and quickly:
it is nearly all money and trinkets ...

But one man has already lost his fine
leather jacket. Bruce Lee, where are you now!
There are dozens of us, just three of them.
As usual, each of us is alone
against the predator, the oppressor ...

For once, even the SAP would do!
When I reach Stepmama's distinctive house
I am too sad to speak, and she sees it.
She serves me tea, strokes my defeated neck.
Her Singer stays, unused, under her bed.

Notes
Tixo! — God!
SAP — South African Police

In the next piece Mtutuzeli Matshoba speaks of 'police reservists' who
often take outrageous advantage of their borrowed authority:

Call Me Not a Man

Mtutuzeli Matshoba

For neither am I a man in the eyes of the law,
Nor am I a man in the eyes of my fellow man.

By dodging, lying, resisting where it is possible, bolting when I'm
already cornered, parting with invaluable money, sometimes calling

my sisters into the game to get amorous with my captors, allowing myself to be slapped on the mouth in front of my womenfolk and getting sworn at with my mother's private parts, that component of me which is man has died countless times in one lifetime. Only a shell of me remains to tell you of the other man's plight, which is in fact my own. For what is suffered by another man in view of my eyes is suffered also by me. The grief he knows is a grief that I know. Out of the same bitter cup do we drink. To the same chain-gang do we belong.

Friday has always been their chosen day to go plundering, although nowadays they come only occasionally, maybe once in a month. Perhaps they have found better pastures elsewhere, where their prey is more predictable than at Mzimhlope, the place which has seen the tragic demise of three of their accomplices who had taken the game a bit too far by entering the hostel on the northern side of our location and fleecing the people right in the midst of their disgusting labour camps. Immediately after this there was a notable abatement in the frequency of their visits to both the location and the adjacent hostel. However the lull was short-lived, lasting only until the storm had died down, because the memory tarnishes quickly in the locations, especially the memory of death. We were beginning to emit sighs of relief and to mutter 'good riddance' when they suddenly reappeared and made their presence in our lives for once again. June, 'seventy-six had put them out of the picture for the next year, during which they were scarcely seen. Like a recurring pestilence they refuse to vanish absolutely from the scene.

A person who has spent some time in Soweto will doubtless have guessed by now that the characters I am referring to are none other than some of the so-called police reservists who roam our dirty streets at weekends, robbing every timid, unsuspecting person, while masquerading as peace officers to maintain law and order in the community. There are no greater thieves than these men of the law, men of justice, peace officers and volunteer public protectors in the whole of the slum complex because, unlike others in the same trade of living off the sweat of their victims, they steal out in the open, in front of everybody's eyes. Of course nothing can be done about it because they go out on their pillaging exploits under the banners of the law, and to rise in protest against them is analogous to defiance of the powers that be.

So, on this Friday too we were standing on top of the station bridge at Mzimhlope. It was about five in the afternoon and the sun hung over the western horizon of spectacularly identical coalsmoke-puffing roof-tops life a gigantic, glowing red ball which dyed the foamy clouds with the crimson sheen of its rays. The commuter trains coming in from the city paused below us every two or three minutes to regurgitate their infinite human cargo, the greater part of whom were hostel-dwellers who hurried up Mohale Street to cook their meagre suppers on primus stoves. The last train we had seen would now be leaving Phefeni, the third station from Mzimhlope. The next train had just emerged from the bridge this side of New Canada, junction to East and West Soweto. The last group of the hostel people from the train now leaving Phefeni had just turned the bend at Mohale Street where it intersects with Elliot. The two hundred metre stretch to Elliot was therefore relatively empty, and people coming towards the station could be clearly made out.

As the wheels of the train from New Canada squealed on the iron tracks and it came to a jerking stop, four men, two in overalls and the others in dustcoats, materialised around the Mohale Street bend. There was no doubt who they were, from the way they filled the whole width of the street and walked as if they owned everything and everybody in their sight. When they came to the grannies selling vegetables, fruit and fried mealies along the ragged, unpaved sides of the street, they grabbed what they fancied and munched gluttonously the rest of the way towards us. Again nothing could be done about it, because the poverty-stricken vendors were not licensed to scrape together some crumbs to ease the gnawing stomachs of their fatherless grandchildren at home, which left them wide open for plunder by the indifferent 'reserves'.

'*Awu*! The Hellions,' remarked Mandla next to me. 'Let's get away from here, my friend'.

He was right. They reminded one of the old western film; but I was not moving from where I was simply because the reservists were coming down the street like a bunch of villains. One other thing I knew was that the railway constable who was on guard duty that Friday at the station did not allow the persecution of the people on his premises. I wanted to have my laugh when they were chased off the station.

'Don't worry about them. Just wait and see how they're going to be chased away by this copper. He won't allow them on the station,' I answered.

They split into twos when they arrived below us. Two of them, a tall chap with a face corroded by skin-lightening cream and wearing a yellow golf cap on his shaven head, and another stubby, shabbily dressed, middle-aged man with a bald frontal lobe and a drunk face, chewing at a cooked sheep's foot that he had taken from one of the grannies, climbed the stairs on our right hand side. The younger

130

man took the flight in fours. The other two chose to waylay their unsuspecting victims on the street corner at the base of the left hand staircase. The first wave of the people who had alighted from the train was in the middle of the bridge when the second man reached the top of the stairs.

Maybe they knew the two reservists by sight, maybe they just smelt cop in the smoggy air, or it being a Friday, they were alert for such possibilities. Three to four of the approaching human wall turned suddenly in their tracks and ran for their dear freedom into the mass behind them. The others were caught unawares by this unexpected movement and they staggered in all directions trying to regain balance. In a split second there was commotion on the station, as if a wild cat had found its way into a fowlrun. Two of those who had not been quick enough were grabbed by their sleeves, and their passes demanded. While they were producing their books the wolves went over their pockets, supposedly feeling for dangerous weapons, dagga and other illegal possessions that might be concealed in the clothes, but really to ascertain whether they had caught the right people for their iniquitous purposes. They were paging through the booklets when the Railway policeman appeared.

'Wha ..? Don't you fools know that you're not supposed to do that shit here? Get off! Get off and do that away from Railway property. Fuck off!' He screamed at the two reservists so furiously that the veins threatened to burst in his neck.

'Arrest the dogs, *baba*! Give them a chance also to taste jail!' Mandla shouted.

'Ja,' I said to Mandla, 'you bet, they've never been where they are so prepared to send others.'

The other people joined in and we jeered the cowards off the station. They descended the stairs with their tails tucked between their legs and joined their companions below the station. Some of the commuters who had been alerted by the uproar returned to the platform to wait there until the reservists had gone before they would dare venture out of the station.

We remained where we had been and watched the persecution from above. I doubted if they even read the passes (if they could), or whether the victims knew if their books were right or out of order. Most likely the poor hunted men believed what they were told by the licensed thieves. The latter demanded the books, after first judging their prey to be weak propositions, flicked through the pages, put the passes into their own pockets, without which the owners could not continue on their way, and told the dumbfounded hostel men to stand aside while they accosted other victims. Within a very short while there was a group of confused men to one side of the street, screaming at their hostel mates to go to room so and so and tell so and so that they had been arrested at the station, and to bring money quickly to release them. Few of those who were being sent heard the messages since they were only too eager to leave the danger zone. Those who had money shook hands with their captors, received their books back and ran up Mohale Street. If they were unlucky they came upon another 'roadblock' three hundred metres up the street where the process was repeated. Woe unto them who had paid their last money to the first extortionists, for this did not matter. The police station was their next stopover before the Bantu Commissioners, and thence their final destination, Modderbee Prison, where they provided the farmers with ready cheap labour until they had served their terms for breaking the law. The terms vary from a few days to two years for *loaferskap*, which is in fact mere un-employment, for which the unfortunate men are not to blame. The whole arrangement stinks of forced labour.

The large *kwela-kwela* swayed down Mohale Street at breakneck speed. The multitudes scattered out of its way and hung onto the sagging fences until it had passed. To be out of sight of the people on the station bridge, it skidded and swerved into the second side street from the station. More reservists poured out of it and went immediately to their dirty job with great zeal. The chain-gang which had been lined up along the fence of the house nearest the station was kicked and shoved to the *kwela-kwela* into which the victims were bundled under a rain of fists and boots, all of them scrambling to go in at the same time through the small door. The driver of the *kwela-kwela*, the only uniformed constable among the group, clanged the door shut and secured it with the locking lever. He went to stand authoritatively near one of the vendors, took a small avocado pear, peeled it and put it whole into a gargantuan mouth, spitting out the large stone later. He did not have to take the trouble of accosting anyone himself. His gangsters would all give him a lion's share of whatever they made, and moreover buy him some beers and brandy. He kept adjusting his polished belt over his potbelly as the 38 police special in its leather holster kept tugging it down. He probably preferred to wear his gun unconventionally, cowboy style.

*

A boy of about seventeen was caught with a knife in his pocket, a dangerous weapon. They slapped him a few times and let him stand handcuffed against the concrete wall of the station. Ten minutes later his well-rounded sister alighted from the train to find her younger brother among the prisoners. As she was inquiring from him why he had been arrested, and reprimanding him for carrying a knife, one of the younger reservists came to stand next to her and started pawing her. She let him carry on, and three minutes later her brother was free. The reservist was beaming all over his face, glad to have won himself a beautiful woman in the course of his duties and little knowing that he had been given the wrong address. Some of our black sisters are at times compelled to go all the way to save their menfolk, and as always, nothing can be done about it.

There was a man coming down Mohale Street, conspicuous amidst the crowd because of the bag and baggage that was loaded on his overall-clad frame. On his right shoulder was a large suitcase with a grey blanket strapped to it with flaxen strings. From his left hand hung a bulging cardboard box, only a few inches from the ground, and tilting him to that side. He walked with the bounce of someone used to walking in gumboots or on uneven ground. There was the urgency of someone who had a long way to travel in his gait. It was doubtless a *goduka* on his way home to his family after many months of work in the city. It might even have been years since he had visited the countryside.

He did not see the hidden *kwela-kwela*, which might have forewarned him of the danger that was lurking at the station. Only when he had stumbled into two reservists, who stepped into his way and ordered him to put down his baggage, did he perhaps remember that it was Friday and raid-day. A baffled expression sprang into his face as he realized what he had walked into. He frantically went through the pockets of his overalls. The worried countenance deepened on his dark face. He tried again to make sure, but he did not find what he was looking for. The men who had stopped him pulled him to one side, each holding him tightly by the sleeve of his overall. He obeyed meekly like a tame animal. They let him lift his arms while they searched him all over the body. Finding nothing hidden on him, they demanded the inevitable book, although they had seen that he did not have it. He gesticulated with his hands as he explained what had caused him not to be carrying his pass with him. A few feet above them, I could hear what was said.

'Strue, *madoda*,' he said imploringly, 'I made a mistake. I luggaged the pass with my trunk. It was in a jacket that I forgot to search before I packed it into the trunk.'

'How do we know that you're not lying?' asked one of the reservists in a querulous voice.

'I'm not lying, *mfowethu*. I swear by my mother, that's what happened,' explained the frightened man.

The second reservist had a more evil and uncompromising attitude.

'That was your own stupidity, mister. Because of it you're going to jail now; no more to your wife.'

'Oh, my brother. Put yourself in my shoes. I've not been home to my people for two years now. It's the first chance I have to go and see my twin daughters who were born while I've been here. Feel for another poor black man, please, my good brother. Forgive me only for this once.'

'What? Forgive you? And don't give us that slush about your children. We've also got our own families, for whom we are at work right now, at this very moment,' the obstinate one replied roughly.

'But, *mfo*. Wouldn't you make a mistake too?'

That was a question the cornered man should not have asked. The reply this time was a resounding slap on the face. 'You think I'm stupid like you, huh? Bind this man, Mazibuko, put the bloody irons on the dog.'

'No, man. Let me talk to the poor bloke. Perhaps he can do something for us in exchange for the favour of letting him proceed on his way home,' the less volatile man suggested, and pulled the hostel man away from the rest of the arrested people.

'*Ja*. Speak to him yourself, Mazibuko. I can't bear talking to rural fools like him. I'll kill him with my bare hands if he thinks that I've come to play here in Johannesburg!' The anger in the man's voice was faked, the fury of a coward trying to instil fear in a person who happened to be at his mercy. I doubted if he could face up to a mouse. He accosted two boys and ran his hands over their sides, but he did not ask for their passes.

'You see, my friend, you're really in trouble. I'm the only one who can help you. This man who arrested you is not in his best mood today. How much have you got on you? Maybe if you give something he'll let you go. You know what wonders money can do for you. I'll plead for you; but only if I show him something can he understand.' The reservist explained the only way out of the predicament for the trapped man, in a smooth voice that sounded rotten through and through with corruption, the sole purpose for which he had joined the 'force'.

'I haven't got a cent in my pocket. I bought provisions, presents for the people at home and the ticket with all the money they gave me at work. Look, *nkosi*, I have only the ticket and the papers with which I'm going to draw my money when I arrive at home.' He took out his papers, pulled the overall off his shoulders and lowered it to his thighs so that the brown trousers he wore underneath were out in the open. He turned the dirty pockets inside out. 'There's nothing else in my pockets except these, mister, honestly.

'Man!'

'Yessir?'

'You want to go home to your wife and children?'

'Yes, please, good man of my people. Give me a break.'

'Then why do you show me these damn papers? They will feed your own children, but not mine. When you get to your home you're going to draw money and your kids will be scratching their tummies and dozing after a hectic meal, while I lose my job for letting you go and my own children join the dogs to scavenge the trashbins. You're mad, *mos*.' He turned to his mate. 'Hey, Baloyi. Your man says he hasn't got anything, but he's going to his family which he hasn't seen for two years.'

'I told you to put the irons on him. He's probably carrying a little fortune in his underpants. Maybe he's shy to take it out in front of the people. It'll come out at the police station, either at the charge office or in the cells when the small boys shake him down.'

'Come on, you. Your hands, maan!'

The other man pulled his arms away from the manacles. His voice rose desperately, '*Awu* my people. You mean you're really arresting me? Forgive me! I pray do.'

A struggle ensued between the two men.

'You're resisting arrest? You — ' and a stream of foul vitriolic words concerning the anatomy of the hostel man's mother gushed out of the reservist's mouth.

'I'm not, I'm not! But please listen!' The hostel man heaved and broke loose from the reservist's grip. The latter was only a lump of fat with nothing underneath. He staggered three steps back and flopped on his rump. When he bounced back to his feet, unexpectedly fast for his bulk, his eyes were blazing murder. His companions came running from their own posts and swarmed upon the defenceless man like a pack of hyenas upon a carcase. The other people who had been marooned on the bridge saw a chance to go past while the wolves were still preoccupied. They ran down the stairs and up Mohale like racehorses. Two other young men who were handcuffed together took advantage of the diversion and bolted down the first street in tandem, taking their bracelets with them. They ran awkwardly with their arms bound together, but both were young and fit and they did their best in the circumstances.

*

We could not stand the sickening beating that the other man was receiving anymore.

'Hey! Hey. *Sies*, maan. Stop beating the man like that. Arrest him if you want to arrest him. You're killing him, dogs!' we protested loudly from the station. An angry crowd was gathering.

'Stop it or we'll stop you from doing anything else forever!' someone shouted.

The psychopaths broke their rugger scrum and allowed us to see their gruesome handiwork. The man was groaning at the base of the fence, across the street where the dirt had gathered. He twisted painfully to a sitting position. His face was covered with dirt and blood from where the manacles that were slipped over the knuckles had found their marks, and his features were grotesquely distorted. In spite of that, the fat man was not satisfied. He bent and gathered the whimpering man's wrists with the intention of fastening them to the fence with the handcuffs.

'Hey, hey, hey, Satan! Let him go. Can't you see that you've hurt that man enough?'

The tension was building up to explosion point and the uniformed policeman sensed it.

'Let him go, boys. Forgive him. Let him go,' he said, shooting nervous glances in all directions.

Then the beaten-up man did the most unexpected and heartrending thing. He knelt before the one ordering his release and held his dust-covered hands with the palms together in the prayer position, and still kneeling he said, 'Thank you very much, my lord. God bless you. Now I can go and see my twins and my people at home.'

He would have done it. Only it never occurred in his mind at that moment of thanksgiving to kiss the red gleaming boots of the policeman.

The miserable man beat the dust off his clothes as best he could, gathered his two parcels and clambered up the stairs, trying to grin his thanks to the crowd that had raised its voice of protest on his behalf. The policemen decided to call it a day. The other unfortunates were shepherded to the waiting *kwela-kwela*.

I tried to imagine how the man would explain his lumps to his wife. In the eye of my mind I saw him throwing his twins into the air and gathering them again and again as he played with them.

'There's still a long way to cover, my friend,' I heard Mandla saying into my ear.

'Before?' I asked.

'Before we reach hell. Ha, ha, ha! Maybe there we'll be men.'

'Ha, we've long been there. We've long been in hell.'

'Before we get out, then.'

136

Notes

baba, or babe — Father or respectful term for an older man

loaferskap — a mixture of English and Afrikaans: the '—skap' can perhaps be translated as '—dom'. If you're black you can be arrested for vagrancy.

kwela-kwela — Police pick-up van. The verb 'kwela' means to climb on or in, to mount.

goduka — a migrant labourer (see note on Mtshali's poem, *Amagoduka at Glencoe Station*)

Madoda — familiar address, abbreviation of 'amadoda', men

mfowethu — my brother

mfo — abbreviation for brother

nkosi — lord, respectful address, 'friend'

In the next story watch how carefully Essop builds the fragility of the relationship between the two characters Rashid and Hazel, in order to have that fragility brutally and humiliatingly shattered by the actions of the two young servicemen:

In the Train

Ahmed Essop

'Hurry Hazel!' he shouted as she raced across the platform towards the carriage door which he held open. He grabbed her outstretched hand as she reached him, pulled her into the carriage as the train began to move. He held her hand firmly and looked at her slender pink-clad perfumed body: her heart was pounding and her breath coming in warm gusts, her whole form a wind-blown anemone.

He had first seen her at the station in Lenasia. She was standing on the platform, a solitary figure looking across the railway lines towards the buildings of the sprawling military camp partly hidden by the foliage of giant blue-gum trees. The morning was fresh and the dew dazzled on the neatly trimmed trees on the platform and the beds of pansies and carnations. His eyes were set ablaze by the bright yellow of her dress and the blue chiffon scarf over her head and knotted under her chin. For a moment he stood still as though some strange communion was established between him and her, a communion at once subtle and clear, and then he lost sight of her as the shrill whistle sounded and commuters rushing towards the opened doors surrounded him.

The next morning he found himself seated opposite her in the carriage. While she turned the pages of a magazine he took the

137

opportunity of looking at her. She was dainty, about fifteen or sixteen years old. Her hair, partly covered by a scarf, was honey-brown in colour; her complexion a tawny sand. And when she raised her eyes as the train stopped to gather more passengers, he saw that they were a greenish grey.

When the train reached Johannesburg he opened the door for her and her 'Thank you' and smile dispelled any diffidence in him. He followed her and asked her where she worked.

'Why, do you want to employ me?' she asked laughingly. And he laughed as accord was established between them.

Every morning Farid went to the station earlier than usual and waited for Hazel's arrival. How his heart frolicked to see her or, when she was late, how it panicked that the train would come and he would have to board it without her. In the train he sat beside her, or opposite her, assured of her presence, involved in her being, and the other passengers seemed vague, undefined dream-forms.

Their love flowered in the train as it sped to Johannesburg. Farid found happiness in little things: in the sight of Hazel's lacquered nails, her squashed handkerchief in her hand, in the brooch that clung to her. And Hazel loved Farid's gaiety, his wit, the gush of words that escaped from his lips.

Farid worked in the office of a property owner. He collected the rent from the tenants and kept records. He left the office at two in the afternoon. Hazel worked in the office of a retailer in Market Street. She lived with her aunt in Lenasia. Her parents were in Cape Town.

Usually the two lovers travelled home in the late afternoon train with the other commuters (Farid having stopped over at ˙friends until it was time to meet Hazel). But there were days when Hazel was not busy in the office and her employer permitted her to leave early. On such days they took the three o'clock train home. The first class compartment in the carriage with its four seats would be empty. The train took forty minutes to reach their destination, and those forty minutes of confinement in a moving carriage were blissful. The carriage became their alcove of love, a mobile alcove untouched by the constantly receding world beyond the windows.

One day when the train reached Mayfair station the carriage door was thrust open and two men in military uniforms entered and sat down on the two vacant seats. The two lovers were puzzled as the carriage was not for whites. The train began to move. Farid and Hazel looked at each other, annoyed that there were others to intrude on their privacy.

Both men were tall, their faces reddened by exposure to the sun.

Their hair, blond and thread-like, was cut very short and one of them had a brush-like moustache. They did not look at Farid or Hazel; they looked at each other, grinning and smirking.

The train gathered momentum. One of the men kicked the other's boot, and the second, suddenly, flung himself onto his partner and held him in a firm embrace. They grimaced and began to bite each other playfully, on the neck, the ears, cheeks. They pushed and jostled, trying to unseat each other. They hugged each other like two large bears — clawing, gripping, twisting and growling. When they were tired from their wrestling they stopped until they had regained their breath. And then they flung themselves on each other again. They fell on the floor and rolled in the limited space, all the time biting and growling like two playful animals. On the floor their wrestling took a different turn — they tried to grab at each other's genitals. They grimaced like puppets. Then one of them seemed to get the better of his fellow and fixed himself to the rear of his partner and performed the motion of coition like a dog.

Farid and Hazel sat mutely, enmeshed.

The two men did not stop in their play until the train began to slow down. By then they were out of breath; their military uniforms no longer spruce, their faces red; but their grimaces remained. As soon as the train came to a halt in Lenasia they jumped out, raced across the platform, jumped down, leaped over the rails and ran towards the military camp.

Farid and Hazel alighted. They walked over the platform without saying a word or holding hands. When they had crossed the overhead bridge and were a short distance away from the station, they began to run.

A 'staffrider' is one who takes a ride on the crowded trains — usually and extremely dangerously on the outside of it. Sometimes this is of necessity (the trains are generally overcrowded); sometimes it is out of sheer bravado:

Staffrider

Motshile Nthodi

> Black boy
> no recreation centre
> no playing grounds

139

no money for lunch at school
not enough schoolbooks
No proper education
no money for school journeys

but
one Saturday morning
my father gave me
one shilling and six pennies
he said
my son
go and make enough
for a living

With eleven pennies
I bought a return ticket to town
the remaining seven for provision
good enough

I was one of those
carry-boys at the municipal market
caddy at the golf course
selling oranges and peanuts
illegally on the trains

money money money
that's not enough for a boy
what about entertainment

right
I am seventeen by now
waiting on a station platform
waiting for the conductor's
whistle of command
waiting for the train
to roll on its permanent rail

now steel wheels of an electric train
start playing a tune of
percussion and trombone
from the middle of the platform
pulling myself from the crowd
waiting for the tube to the north

like a bebop dancer
I turn around twice
and I open the window
push up the frame with my elbow
grab the frame between
the window and the door

listen to the improvisation
from my dirty oversize
canvas shoes
pha − − phapha − phapha −
pha − phapha − phapha−
phapha − phapha −

listen to the shouting
and whistles
from the audience in that tube
when I swing on the outer handle
and rest on the bottom stair

THAT'S THEATRE HEY

they see me once
but only once
I'm on top of the coach
lying eight inches under
the main power lines

ACROBATIC HEY

they see me once again
but only once
I'm under the coach
lying on a steel frame
next to the wheels

CIRCUS HEY

fifteen stations
stupids packed
sardines in the tube
phapha − pha −
poor black eyes on me

        — phapha —
        home station
        — pha — phapha — phaphaphaphapha

        WA SALA WENA

        — phaphapha —
        railway police chasing me
        I jump the platform
        the railway line
        the fence
        across the river
        towards home
        I'm safe

        this is the Saturday programme
        and till we meet again
        thank you brothers and sisters,
        thank you.

Notes
Wa sala wena — You, stay!

Points for discussion

- It is clear that Mzamane's DUBE TRAIN REVISITED is a respectful bow in the direction of Can Themba's THE DUBE TRAIN: Mzamane's piece is even dedicated to Themba. Can you see the debt the younger writer owes the older? Have things changed much? In what ways?
- Is the last line of Johennesse's THE NIGHT TRAIN a surprise when it comes? It seems so self-involved a poem, so concerned with the individual, that an emotion like fear, necessarily involving something outside of the poet, seems strangely at odds. But why is this revelation completely convincing?
- A very personable and engaging character comes across to us in BYE BYE, OVERCOAT. Do you wish he'd been more aggressive, less resigned, less accepting of so bad a situation? He seems to reject the obviously heroic himself ('Bruce Lee, where are you now?') — but would you have wanted him to put up more of a show against the train thuggery?
- Mtutuzeli Matshoba's stories all throw into relief the real violence of much township life. But the violence is the 'institutionalized violence' of

142

a system rather than any innate violence in the people. What do you think is meant by this? And how does this story show it?

- There's no doubt that the kind of incident in IN THE TRAIN could happen, stunning and shocking as it is in its violation of people's privacy and dignity. What motivates the two young men to behave this way in public? Would they ever have behaved this way if the other two occupants of the compartment had been white? And what does this imply about the stage things have got to in South Africa? How 'real' is the last sentence of the story: is that how you imagine Farid and Hazel would have reacted.?

- What an explosion of exuberance and playfulness Nthodi's poem STAFFRIDER is! What do you think of the jazz-improvization of the 'pha — phapha — . . .' etc.? Do you understand why the 17-year-old boy does not want to be one of the 'stupids packed sardines'?

'Die Ore' — Encounters with the police

I am not sure why the South African Police earned this nickname, 'The Ears'. Could it be that their ears show fairly prominently below their caps, with their 'short back and sides' haircuts? Or could it be as prosaic as a corruption of the prison term for warders, 'boere'?

Riot

Casey Motsisi

Maria Mbatha looked at the clock on the kitchen dresser. The clock had stopped. But she knew instinctively that it was very late at night and her eyes were heavy with sleep. She yawned as she continued to rock the young boy she was carrying in her arms to sleep.

But the boy kept staring unblinkingly into the dim-lit room with big, sleepless eyes. They both listened to the noisy silence of the room.

'Ma,' the young boy said softly.

'Yes, my son.' Her mind was still blank.

'Ma, I want water.'

'Water.' She repeated the word like a child learning a new word at school.

'Ma, I want water, water, water,' he rattled.

'Shut up, you're making noise. Why don't you wait for your mother to come and give you water?'

'I want water. I want water. Put me down. I want water.'

The palm of her hand came down hard on the young boy's buttocks. He did not cry. He started kicking his feet up and down.

'Next time I will make you feel the sjambok, Boetikie,' she vowed after the young boy's fist had caught her smartly on the chin.

'I want water. Put me down. I want water...'

Maria, still holding the young boy in one hand, stood up and gave him a mug full of water. 'You just wet the blankets tonight and see what happens to you tomorrow,' she said as she watched him gulp the water greedily.

'Ma, I'm hungry,' Boetikie said after finishing the water.

'You must be mad. You had food during the day. You think I'm here to work for you as if you are a European?' She carried him over to the bed and tucked him in.

'I don't want to sleep. I want food. I'm hungry.'

'Shut up now. Don't act like a lunatic. One of these days I will kill you, Boetikie, God in Heaven hears me.'

Boetikie pulled the blanket and covered his head. Maria stood looking at the covered heap for a while. She shook her head and went outside.

Outside, Western Township lay sleeping restlessly under an over-cast sky. Usually, at this late hour on Sundays, Western Township, like most African townships, would be alive with drunken revellers staggering home from shebeens and 'midnight parties'.

But tonight, like the past few Sundays, Western was quiet. Yet one could not fail to miss the undercurrent of restlessness that throbbed through the belly of the township. When will it ever end? 'I hate this boycott,' Maria cursed softly, bitterly, and went back into the room.

Boetikie was snoring nasally. She felt relieved that he was asleep. How this child gets on my nerves! But there was no anger or bitterness in her thoughts. Boetikie was all she had in the world. Her husband had been killed during a faction fight between 'Russians' in neighbouring Newclare.

Nana, their only daughter, was married and was now staying in Port Elizabeth. Boetikie was Nana's child but Maria had to look after him because the man who married Nana did not want the child to live with them.

Maria went to the stove and pulled out the ashtin. There was a bottle in it. She took it out, poured some of the liquid into a glass and gulped it down. Her face contorted into a mask of agony as the brandy burned her throat and warmed her stomach. She sat on a chair and placed the brandy on the table. She stared at the half-empty bottle, hating it and loving it at the same time. She wondered what her husband would have said if he had caught her drinking.

Maria squeezed her head with both hands. Her head was bursting with pain. She felt as though parts of it were falling away in pieces.

She seized the bottle and poured herself another tot.

After gulping it down she felt the pain filtering out of her head, leaving a delicious sensation that was a mixture of dare and bravado.

Suddenly the world became a wonderful and beautiful thing and she began to mumble a song. She was now falling in love with the world she had hated so passionately a few hours ago. She thought of the long walk she would have to make the following day to fetch the bundle of washing in town. For tomorrow would be Monday — 'Washing Day'. Although she was not feeling tired, she told herself that she would not go to town. 'To hell with the boycott and the washing!'

It felt comforting to be able to say that. It made her feel like a person, a human being who has a right to live her own life the way she wanted to live it.

'Azikhwelwa!' she shouted. 'We won't board the buses,' she interpreted for herself. Just like at the meetings. She laughed and poured herself another shot. Then another. And yet another. After a while followed blissful unconsciousness.

She fell asleep on the table, holding the bottle in one hand and the glass in the other.

A slight breeze trickled through a crack in one of the panes of the window behind Maria's back. The flame of the cigarette-high candle that was stuck in a saucer, flickered for a moment, as if struggling to hold its own against the breeze. But the breeze licked it off the wick and muffled it in its coldness. The room was now in semi-darkness.

Maria's body rose and fell rhythmically with her heavy breathing. As it rose, it seemed to swell with all the pride and joy that had filled the brief years when she had her husband and the crowning glory she felt when she gave birth to their only child, Nana. She had seen her grow into a fine woman.

And as it fell, it was as if all her forty-five years of frustration were weighing heavily down on her plump body, battling to drain the life out of her.

Maria slept, her mind steeped in the uncaring abandon of the drunk.

Peaceful. No thoughts; no dreams; no hopes nor fears of tomorrow. Bottle-kind of peace, but peace all the same. And the township also slept, nestled uneasily between the inflammable Sophiatown to the north and the lusty Newclare to the south. On the east was Coronationville, prim and pretentious. And on the west, Nature, grim and sad, licking at the scars, dongas, inflicted on her by man with the sharp spades of civilisation.

Morning crept stealthily into Maria's room, like a policeman stalking a dangerous, armed tsotsi. Maria felt the nursemaid of the mind silently drawing the curtains of sleep away from her eyes. Slowly, she drifted back into wakefulness, but her eyes refused to open. Her head throbbed with a clanging pain.

She knew the pain. A hangover. A hangover coupled with the effects of drinking heavily on an empty stomach. She rubbed her eyes and realised that the door was slightly open. She remembered that she had not locked it last night. The thought that she had slept without locking the door sent a shiver of fright through her spine.

Then she felt someone shaking her rudely on the shoulder.

'Come on, woman. Don't waste my time. I'm arresting you.'

She looked up. Beside her stood a khaki-clad, hefty man. The Law! And in one hand The Law held a bottle of brandy and in the other The Law held a glass. Maria recognised them as her own.

Maria stood up. She was an inch or two taller than The Law. She looked at The Law, feeling sick and scared; cringing and confused.

'Come, woman, let's go,' The Law commanded authoritatively.

'Please, father policeman,' Maria pleaded. 'Don't arrest me, I have to go to work ... and I ... please, father policeman ...'

But Maria knew that it was no use trying to plead with The Law. She had always regarded the police as sub-humans, people without compassion and feeling. People who found untold joy in life by arresting, bullying and manhandling others. She heard other policemen shouting and cursing outside. The police were everywhere. It was a raid.

She heard a woman protesting and recognized the voice. It was MaSello, her next-door neighbour. 'Don't hit my son like that! I will bring you before the court.'

'He has no pass and he's cheeky. These educated tsotsis! He says I have no right to ask him for a pass when he's in bed. Who does he think he is? I'll knock the education out of his head, I vow by my mother.'

Maria had resigned herself to the worst. She could not even believe her ears when the policeman gave her back the bottle of brandy and told her to hide it. 'Quickly, woman. Hide it before I change my mind.'

Maria snatched the bottle and shoved it into the ashtin of the stove. 'I don't know when I'll become a Sergeant, doing such stupid things,' she heard the policeman mumble as he went out of the house. He banged the door so hard the house rattled with the impact.

The noise woke up Boetikie with a start. Maria, although she could not say why, was crying softly.

'Ma, you're crying.'

'Yes, my son,' she sniffed.

'Why, Ma?'

'Oh, sheddup!'

When Maria came back from town in the afternoon, carrying a bundle of soiled washing on her head, she was still bitter at the experience she had had at the bus stop. Because she was tired from walking all the way to town, she had boarded the Coronationville bus as these buses were not affected by the fare increase which sparked off the Bus Boycott.

A young Coloured boy had constantly bumped her and called her all sorts of names to unsettle her. But Maria had managed to keep cool.

She met MaSello outside. 'MaSello, did you send Boetikie to the shop?' she asked.

'No,' said MaSello. 'But I saw him running with MaBatho's son towards Sophiatown. There's a fight there, you know. The people are stoning the buses and trains and cars. I understand that one of the buses from town — and it was empty, mark you — ran over an old man who was crossing the main road. That's why the people are stoning the buses.'

MaSello had hardly finished her narrative and Maria was dashing full throttle in the direction of Sophiatown.

Fear exploded in every pore of her body. She stumbled, fell and scrambled to her feet again, all the while calling Boetikie's name.

A few yards away from the trellis that divided Sophiatown from Western Township, she realised the full impact of the riot. There was screaming and shouting. People of all shapes and sizes were scampering up and down the streets.

And the police, from nearby Newlands Police Station, fired their guns and pistols above the heads of the milling mob.

Maria had seen Sophiatown many a time in an ugly mood. But today Sophiatown looked like a city at war. There were people lying wounded or dead along the tram rails and the main street.

A policeman, leading two children, a boy and a girl, by the hands, crossed over into Western Township through an opening in the trellis.

Maria realised that the boy was Boetikie. With a shout of joy and relief, she ran towards the policeman. 'Save my child, save my child!' she shouted hysterically.

Just at the moment, a group of women and young tsotsis who had been witnessing the little war from a safe distance, mobbed the policeman.

'What are you doing to our children, you government dog?' one of the women shrieked. In a moment the women were upon him, clawing at him, tearing his khaki uniform and battering his head with stones held firmly in their hands. He fell and everybody disappeared.

As Maria pulled Boetikie away she saw the face of the policeman. Something knotted inside her as if to squeeze all the water from her system and bring it out silently through her eyes.

When she reached home the shooting had lulled. A spasmodic 'boom' here and there after long intervals.

That night, Maria and Boetikie went to bed without having supper. She did not feel hungry and even Boetikie had not asked for food. It took her a long time to fall asleep. She just lay in the darkness of the locked and bolted room and listened to the whine of ambulances that made the dark room even more foreboding.

And she thought of a policeman whose body was perhaps still lying cold and stoned and punctured along the trellis. She choked and wept.

. . . Only that same morning that policeman had been alive. That same policeman had been in her room asking her to hide the bottle of brandy. If he had arrested her, she thought, then she would not be remembering his young, pinkish face lying dead and uncared for along the trellis that divides Western Township from Sophiatown . . .

Notes

sjambok — a hide whip or strap
boetikie — Afrikaans: a diminutive of 'boetie' (brother) which is itself already a diminutive of 'boet', the abbreviation of 'broeder'
Azikhwelwa — The slogan of the bus boycott: 'We will not climb on!'

Hats Off In My House!

Sipho Sepamla

> my old man
> he was a drinking father
> he had a brother
> he was a drinking uncle
> they had a darling sister
> ooo! she was a drinking old mate

come some day
in walked a young constable
who saw very soon
everyone was pissed like a sailor

now anyone will tell you
there's nothing like a law agent
for straightaway the little constable
fixed his authority

in that instant
my sometimes pugnacious old man
he who was an incorrigible guzzler
saw fit to spit at the law
and hands raised to God shouted
hats off in my house!

the poor little constable
as if he had forgotten his law
was terribly, terribly deflated
he retraced his dubious step
amid the clinking of glasses and bottles
and words clapping the air freely

fast as their courage returned
my bloody relations
all spat in staccato
blabbering in the name of justice
the rights of the individual

ooo! I can't tell all I felt
on that memorable day
as I saw happily
my proud family of guzzlers
taking the law into their own hands.

A Riot Policeman

Chris van Wyk

The sun has gone down
with the last doused flame.
Tonight's last bullet
has singed the day's last victim
an hour ago.
It is time to go home.

The hippo crawls
in a desultory air of triumph
through, around fluttering
shirts and shoes full of death.
Teargas is simmering.
Tears have been dried by heat
or cooled by death.
Buckshot fills the space
between the maimed and the mourners.
It is time to go home.

A black man surrenders
a stolen bottle of brandy
scurries away with his life
in his hands.
The policeman rests the oasis
on his lips
wipes his mouth on a camouflaged
cuff.
It is time to go home.

Tonight he'll shed his uniform.
Put on his pyjamas.
Play with his children.
Make love to his wife.
Tomorrow is pay-day.
But it is time to go home now,
It is time to go home.

Notes

hippo — a slang term for an armoured police vehicle

151

The next piece is an extract from the speech Alan Paton made at the last public meeting of the Liberal Party, held in Durban in May 1968. The Liberal Party was disbanded when the government forbade multi-racial political parties.

Words to the Security Police

Alan Paton

I should like first to take this opportunity of saying a few words to the members of the security police. These words will not be insulting, they will merely be truthful. I do not know if this is my farewell to the security police or whether we shall meet again. I used to pretend — I suppose it was my duty to pretend — that it was nothing to me to be watched by you, and to be followed by you, and to have my telephone conversations listened to by you, and to have some of my letters — I do not say all of them — read by you, and to have my house searched by you, and to have you sitting in a car outside my house so that all my neighbours could see what kind of person I was. But I was only pretending. After fifty years of a life blameless in the eyes of the law, it was painful suddenly to become the object of the attention of the security police of my own country, to fly to Johannesburg to find you waiting for me at the airport, to fly to Cape Town and find you there too. I am by nature a private rather than a public man, and this attention was painful to me.

Though this is a sad occasion for the Liberal Party of South Africa, it is of course a triumphant occasion for you, for you have carried out successfully the task allotted to you. You have advised the Minister to restrict the freedom of many of our leading members. I shall mention only two of these. I shall mention the name of Miss Heather Morkill in Pietermaritzburg and Mrs Jean Hill in Durban, who are people I can only describe as good, brave and honourable women, and it is a sick country and a sick government that must restrict the freedom of people who are good and brave and honourable.

The person who smashed my car window at the Hogsback did not have his freedom restricted. But of course there may be a good reason for that, namely that his identity was never discovered. And there may be a bad reason for it too, namely that his identity was never revealed.

My relationship with you has had its happier moments. Once

when we were holding a meeting at my house you came and parked in the street outside. And I went out and said to you, 'You are welcome to come and park in the garden, and you will be able better to see what is going on,' to which you replied, 'Mr Paton, are we embarrassing you?' And I said, 'Yes you are.' And you said, 'Well, we'll go and park somewhere else.' And I said, 'Thank you.'

There was one funny moment too. When you came in 1966 to search my house, you came into the writing-room, and one of you said to the others, *'God, man, die boeke!'* And there was another high point too. You asked me to take you to my study, where there were still more books and papers, and I did so, and I said to you, 'Gentlemen, you may take my word or not, but I tell you that this is where I do my literary work when I do any literary work, and that there are no political papers here,' whereupon you took my word and did not search my study. Thus was never discovered my fiendish plot to blow up Parliament, and all the parliamentarians except the ones I fancied. I hope of course that these revelations of mine will not get any of you into trouble.

But there were other things not quite so happy or funny. Why did one of our leading members have to be arrested at a funeral? Why did a train have to be stopped in the middle of the veld, and one of our members arrested in full view of all the passengers, when you had seen him openly moving about on the platform at the previous station? Why did an old mother have to be visited, and warned that she would be destitute if her son persisted in being a member of the Liberal Party?

I hope you do not mind my addressing you thus. I have no wish to treat you discourteously. But for fifteen years you have been, not exactly our comrades, but closer to us than brothers. You will say to me, *'We have a job to do,'* and I shall say to you, *'Thank God I don't have to do it.'*

Notes
God, man, die boeke — God, man, the books!

Points for discussion
- The first story portrays an individual white policeman in a surprisingly good light. Surely no stronger animosity exists than that created, set up and established by the South African authorities, between the white police force and the black people. So is this writer telling us that there is a largeness of spirit in individual people that can overwhelm — maybe

even destroy — what has been so consciously set up? What are your feelings about this? What do you feel about the policeman in the story, and about the black protagonist? Do you take issue with my use of the word 'surprisingly', or with my specifying the police as white and the people as black, when clearly there are also black police and white people?

- What a splendid reprimand Sepamla's father brings down on the head of the 'poor little constable' in HATS OFF IN MY HOUSE! It's the kind of gesture that makes you want to cheer and applaud spontaneously. Do you think Sepamla has given anything away by his title?

- The view of the police given in the poem A RIOT POLICEMAN is different from that given in the first story of this section. There's a time difference to be noted. The story was written before 16 June 1976. The events of that time and the actions of the police changed everything. The poem was written after 1976, and so attitudes have understandably hardened. Can you make the imaginative leap van Wyk has asked? Can you imagine the stereotype of the South African policeman in his pyjamas, playing with his children, making love to his wife?

- Alan Paton was a great stylist. Even here in a speech given at an emotional time, how balanced and poised the sentences are. The structure is direct and simple: no unnecessary words or convoluted phrasings. It speaks straight and direct and unadorned — just what's required in the circumstance.

Inside

It is an unhappy commentary on South Africa that a considerable body of prison literature now exists. Most of the pieces that follow concern 'politicals', people in prison as a result of their political convictions and actions.

While Dennis Brutus was in prison on Robben Island he smuggled poems out to his wife, apparently written on toilet paper:

Letters to Martha 4

Dennis Brutus

> Particularly in a single cell,
> but even in the sections
> the religious sense asserts itself;
>
> perhaps a childhood habit of nightly prayers
> the accessibility of Bibles,
> or awareness of the proximity of death:
>
> and, of course, it is a currency —
> pietistic expressions can purchase favours
> and it is a way of suggesting reformation
> (which can procure promotion);
>
> and the resort of the weak
> is to invoke divine revenge
> against a rampaging injustice;

but in the grey silence of the empty afternoons
it is not uncommon
to find oneself talking to God.

Letters to Martha 9

Dennis Brutus

The not-knowing
is perhaps the worst part of the agony
for those outside:

not knowing what cruelties must be endured
what indignities the sensitive spirit must face
what wounds the mind can be made to inflict
on itself;

and the hunger to be thought of
to be remembered
and to reach across space
with filaments of tenderness
and consolation.

And knowledge.
even when it is knowledge of ugliness
seems to be preferable,
can be better endured.

And so,
for your consolation
I send these fragments,
random pebbles I pick up
from the landscape of my own experience,
traversing the same arid wastes
in a montage of glimpses
I allow myself
or stumble across.

Letters to Martha 10

Dennis Brutus

It is not all terror
and deprivation,
you know;

one comes to welcome the closer contact
and understanding one achieves
with one's fellow-men,
fellows, compeers;

and the discipline does much to force
a shape and pattern on one's daily life
as well as on the days

and honest toil
offers some redeeming hours
for the wasted years;

so there are times
when the mind is bright and restful
though alive:
rather like the full calm morning sea.

Letters to Martha 18

Dennis Brutus

I remember rising one night
after midnight
and moving
through an impulse of loneliness
to try and find the stars.

And through the haze
the battens of fluorescents made
I saw pinpricks of white
I thought were stars.

157

Greatly daring
I thrust my arm through the bars
and easing the switch in the corridor
plunged my cell in darkness

I scampered to the window
and saw the splashes of light
where the stars flowered.

But through my delight
thudded the anxious boots
and a warning barked
from the machine-gun post
on the catwalk.

And it is the brusque inquiry
and threat
that I remember of that night
rather than the stars.

Walking on Air

Jeremy Cronin

Prologue

In the prison workshop, also known as the seminar
    room;

In the seminar room, sawdust up the nose, feet in plane shavings,
    old jam tins on racks, a dropped plank, planks, a stack of mason's
    floats waiting assembly, Warder von Loggerenberg sitting in the
    corner;

In the prison workshop, also and otherwise named, where work is
    done by enforced dosage, between political discussion, theoretical
    discussion, tactical discussion, bemoaning of life without women,
    sawdust up the nose, while raging at bench 4, for a week long, a
    discussion raging, above the hum of the exhaust fans, on how to
    distinguish the concept 'Productive' from the concept . . . 'Unpro-
    ductive Labour';

In the prison workshop, then, over the months, over the screech of the grindstone, I'm asking John Matthews about his life and times, as I crank the handle, he's sharpening a plane blade, holding it up in the light to check on its bevel, dipping the blade to cool in a tin of water, then back to the grindstone, sparks fly: 'I work for myself' — he says — 'not for the boere';

In the prison workshop, with John Matthews making contraband goeters, boxes, ashtrays, smokkel salt cellars of, oh, delicate dove-tailings;

Over the months, then, in the prison workshop, I'm asking John Matthews, while he works intently, he likes manual work, he likes the feel of woodgrain, he doesn't like talking too much, the making and fixing of things he likes, he likes, agh no, hayikona, slap-bang-bang, work for the jailers;

In the prison workshop, then, I ask John Matthews, was he present on the two days of Kliptown ... 1955? ... when the People's Congress adopted the Freedom Charter?

Actually

No he wasn't

He was there the day before, he built the platform

In the prison workshop, then, over the hum of exhaust fans, between the knocking in of nails, the concept 'Productive', the concept 'Unproductive Labour', feet in plane shavings, John Matthews speaks by snatches, the making and fixing of things he likes, though much, never, much you won't catch him speaking:

But here, pieced together, here from many months, from the prison workshop

Here is one comrade's story.

*

Born to Bez Valley, Joburg
into the last of his jail term
stooped now he has grown

In this undernourished frame
that dates back
to those first years of his life.

He was nine
when his father came
blacklisted home

From the 1922
Rand Revolt,
and there with a makeshift

Forge in their backyard
a never again to be employed
father passed on to his son

A lifelong
love for the making
and fixing of things.

From Bez Valley it was,
veiled like a bride in fine
mine-dump dust

He went out
to whom it may concern
comma

A dependable lad
comma
his spelling is good.

At fifteen he became
office boy at Katzenellenbogen's
cnr. von Wielligh

And President streets
where he earned: £1 a week,
where he learned:

*Good spelling doesn't always count.
*The GPO telegram charge is reckoned per word.
*A word is 15 letters max.
*You have to drop ONE *l* from Katzenellenbogen Inc or
                    HEAR ME BOY?! nex' time
                    YOU'S gonna pay extra one word
                    charge your bliksem self.

And the recession came
but he got a bookkeeping job
with Kobe Silk

On the same block
— John Edward
Matthews

Mondays to Fridays
on that same block
for 37 unbroken years until

The security police
picked him up ... But first
way back to the thirties.

WEEKENDS IN THE THIRTIES:
church and picnics
by Zoo Lake.

And later, deedle-deedle
— Dulcie, heel-toe,
his future wife

Whom he courted with
(he can still do it)
diddle-diddle: the cake-walk

And always
on Sundays it was
church and church

And then to Kobe Silk
there came
a new clerk

Myer Chames by name
a short little bugger who talked
Economics at lunch-break

And Myer Chames talked
of all hitherto existing societies,
the history of freeman

And slave, lord, serf,
guildmaster, journeyman,
bourgeois, proletarian and

In a word
John Matthews stopped
going to church.

His name got inscribed
inside
of a red party card.

He'd sell Inkululekos down by
Jeppestown
Friday nights

While the bourgeois press wrote
    RUSSIA HAS GONE SOFT ON HITLER
He learnt to fix duplicators and typewriters.

He was still selling
Inkululekos in 1943
when even the bourgeois press wrote

RED ARMY HAS BROKEN
BROKEN
THE BACK OF HITLER

In the year 1943 − born
to Dulcie and John
a daughter

Their first child
first of seven.
And now

Into the last months
of his 15 years
prison term

At nights in his cell
he peeps down at his face
in a mirror

In a mirror held low, about
belly-height
wondering how he'll seem

To his grandchildren
from down there
next year when he comes out.

But that's later ... back
to 1950
The Suppression of Communism Act

Membership becomes a punishable crime.
But laws only
postpone matters − somewhat.

There were still duplicators to fix
and typewriters to mend
through the 50s

Passive Resistance, the Congress Alliance,
    Defiance Campaign, Pass Burnings, Bus
    Boycott, Potato Boycott, the Women's
    March, the Treason Trial, the Freedom
    Charter, until

Until 1960: the massacre
    Sharpeville
        and Langa.

And people said: 'Enough,
our patience, it has limits' ... and so
it was no longer just typewriters and duplicators
                                to mend.
A man would come to the backyard and whisper:
                        30 ignitors.
And John Matthews would make 30, to be
                        delivered to X.
And a man would come in the dead of night
These need storing comrade, some things
                    wrapped in waterproof cloth.
        TERRORISTS BOMB POWERLINES
He would read in the bourgeois press, or

163

MIDNIGHT PASS OFFICE BLAST

He'd sigh a small sigh
— Hadn't been sure
Those damned ignitors would work.

Finally.
1964.
After a quarter century in the struggle

A security police swoop
and John Matthews was one
among several detained.

White and 52
so they treated him nice.
They only made him stand

On two bricks
for three days
and three nights and

When he asked to go to the lavatory
they said:
            Shit in your pants.

But the State needed witnesses
So they changed their tune.
Tried sweet-talking him round.
Think of your career
      (that didn't work)
Think of the shame of going to jail
      (that thought only
      filled him with pride)
You really want kaffirs to rule?
      (like you said)
Think of your wife
      (Dulcie. Dulcie.
      7 kids. Dulcie.
      She's not political at all).

And there they had him.
On that score he was worried, it's true.
And they promised him freedom.

And they pressed him for weeks on end.
Until finally he said:

Okay, agreed.

— But first I must speak with my wife.

Barely an hour it took them to find
and rush Dulcie Matthews
out to Pretoria Jail.

Then looking nice, because they let him shave,
let him comb his hair, looking nice then, chaperoned by
smiling, matrimonial policemen, shaven and combed, John
Matthews got led out to his wife, and holding her hand, they
let him hold her hand, he said
— Do you know why they've brought you?
And she said
— I do.
And he said
— Dulcie, I will never betray my comrades.
And with a frog in her throat she replied
— I'm behind you. One hundred percent.

So back they hauled John Matthews then and there,

back to the cells,
that was that, then, but
all the way down the passage
toe-heel, heel-toe, diddle-diddle
ONE HUNDRED PERCENT
I mean, he was high
off the ground, man.

He was walking on air.

Notes

boere — Afrikaans: literally farmers, but broadened in meaning to include all
    Afrikaners. In prison jargon this is again narrowed down to 'the warders'
goeters — slang term for 'goods and chattels, belongings, bits and pieces'
    (Branford Dictionary)
smokkel — smuggled in
hayikona (or aikona) — 'an emphatic negative "never!" or "not on your life!"'
    (Branford Dictionary)

165

bliksem — 'an abusive mode of address (or reference) to someone, roughly
equivalent to "bastard", "blackguard" ' (Branford Dictionary)
Inkululeko — literally, freedom; here used as the name of a workers' newspaper

The Prisoner Who Wore Glasses

Bessie Head

Scarcely a breath of wind disturbed the stillness of the day and the
long rows of cabbages were bright green in the sunlight. Large white
clouds drifted slowly across the deep blue sky. Now and then they
obscured the sun and caused a chill on the backs of the prisoners
who had to work all day long in the cabbage field. This trick the
clouds were playing with the sun eventually caused one of the
prisoners who wore glasses to stop work, straighten up and peer
short-sightedly at them. He was a thin little fellow with a hollowed-
out chest and comic knobbly knees. He also had a lot of fanciful
ideas because he smiled at the clouds.

'Perhaps they want me to send a message to the children,' he
thought, tenderly, noting that the clouds were drifting in the direction
of his home some hundred miles away. But before he could frame
the message, the warder in charge of his work span shouted: 'Hey,
what you tink you're doing, Brille?'

The prisoner swung round, blinking rapidly, yet at the same time
sizing up the enemy. He was a new warder, named Jacobus Stephanus
Hannetjie. His eyes were the colour of the sky but they were
frightening. A simple, primitive, brutal soul gazed out of them. The
prisoner bent down quickly and a message was quietly passed down
the line: 'We're in for trouble this time, comrades.'

'Why?' rippled back up the line.

'Because he's not human,' the reply rippled down and yet only
the crunching of the spades as they turned over the earth disturbed
the stillness.

This particular work span was known as Span One. It was composed
of ten men and they were all political prisoners. They were grouped
together for convenience as it was one of the prison regulations
that no black warder should be in charge of a political prisoner lest
this prisoner convert him to his views. It never seemed to occur to
the authorities that this very reasoning was the strength of Span One
and a clue to the strange terror they aroused in the warders. As
political prisoners they were unlike the other prisoners in the sense

166

that they felt no guilt nor were they outcasts of society. All guilty men instinctively cower, which was why it was the kind of prison where men got knocked out cold with a blow at the back of the head from an iron bar. Up until the arrival of Warder Hannetjie, no warder had dared beat any member of Span One and no warder had lasted more than a week with them. The battle was entirely psychological. Span One was assertive and it was beyond the scope of white warders to handle assertive black men. Thus, Span One had got out of control. They were the best thieves and liars in the camp. They lived all day on raw cabbages. They chatted and smoked tobacco. And since they moved, thought and acted as one, they had perfected every technique of group concealment.

Trouble began that very day between Span One and Warder Hannetjie. It was because of the short-sightedness of Brille. That was the nickname he was given in prison and is the Afrikaans word for someone who wears glasses. Brille could never judge the approach of the prison gates and on several previous occasions he had munched on cabbages and dropped them almost at the feet of the warder and all previous warders had overlooked this. Not so Warder Hannetjie.

'Who dropped that cabbage?' he thundered.

Brille stepped out of line.

'I did,' he said meekly.

'Alright,' said Hannetjie. 'The whole Span goes three meals off.'

'But I told you I did it,' Brille protested.

The blood rushed to Warder Hannetjie's face.

'Look 'ere,' he said. 'I don't take orders from a kaffir. I don't know what kind of kaffir you tink you are. Why don't you say Baas? I'm your Baas. Why don't you say Baas, hey?'

Brille blinked his eyes rapidly but by contrast his voice was strangely calm.

'I'm twenty years older than you,' he said. It was the first thing that came to mind but the comrades seemed to think it a huge joke. A titter swept up the line. The next thing Warder Hannetjie whipped out a knobkerrie and gave Brille several blows about the head. What surprised his comrades was the speed with which Brille had removed his glasses or else they would have been smashed to pieces on the ground.

That evening in the cell Brille was very apologetic.

'I'm sorry, comrades,' he said. 'I've put you into a hell of a mess.'

'Never mind, brother,' they said. 'What happens to one of us, happens to all.'

'I'll try to make up for it, comrades,' he said. 'I'll steal something so that you don't go hungry.'

Privately, Brille was very philosophical about his head wounds. It was the first time an act of violence had been perpetrated against him but he had long been a witness of extreme, almost unbelievable human brutality. He had twelve children and his mind travelled back that evening through the sixteen years of bedlam in which he had lived. It had all happened in a small drab little three-bedroomed house in a small drab little street in the Eastern Cape and the children kept coming year after year because neither he nor Martha ever managed the contraceptives the right way and a teacher's salary never allowed moving to a bigger house and he was always taking exams to improve his salary only to have it all eaten up by hungry mouths. Everything was pretty horrible, especially the way the children fought. They'd get hold of each other's heads and give them a good bashing against the wall. Martha gave up somewhere along the line so they worked out a thing between them. The bashings, biting and blood were to operate in full swing until he came home. He was to be the bogey-man and when it worked he never failed to have a sense of godhead at the way in which his presence could change savages into fairly reasonable human beings.

Yet somehow it was this chaos and mismanagement at the centre of his life that drove him into politics. It was really an ordered beautiful world with just a few basic slogans to learn along with the rights of mankind. At one stage, before things became very bad, there were conferences to attend, all very far away from home.

'Let's face it,' he thought ruefully. 'I'm only learning right now what it means to be a politician. All this while I've been running away from Martha and the kids.'

And the pain in his head brought a hard lump to his throat. That was what the children did to each other daily and Martha wasn't managing and if Warder Hannetjie had not interrupted him that morning he would have sent the following message: 'Be good comrades, my children. Co-operate, then life will run smoothly.'

The next day Warder Hannetjie caught this old man of twelve children stealing grapes from the farm shed. They were an enormous quantity of grapes in a ten gallon tin and for this misdeed the old man spent a week in the isolation cell. In fact, Span One as a whole was in constant trouble. Warder Hannetjie seemed to have eyes at the back of his head. He uncovered the trick about the cabbages, how they were split in two with the spade and immediately covered with earth and then unearthed again and eaten with split-second timing. He found out how tobacco smoke was beaten into the ground and he found out how conversations were whispered down the wind.

168

For about two weeks Span One lived in acute misery. The cabbages, tobacco and conversations had been the pivot of jail life to them. Then one evening they noticed that their good old comrade who wore the glasses was looking rather pleased with himself. He pulled out a four ounce packet of tobacco by way of explanation and the comrades fell upon it with great greed. Brille merely smiled. After all, he was the father of many children. But when the last shred had disappeared, it occured to the comrades that they ought to be puzzled. Someone said: 'I say, brother. We're watched like hawks these days. Where did you get the tobacco?'

'Hannetjie gave it to me,' said Brille.

There was a long silence. Into it dropped a quiet bombshell.

'I saw Hannetjie in the shed today,' and the failing eyesight blinked rapidly. 'I caught him in the act of stealing five bags of fertilizer and he bribed me to keep my mouth shut.'

There was another long silence.

'Prison is an evil life,' Brille continued, apparently discussing some irrelevant matter. 'It makes a man contemplate all kinds of evil deeds.'

He held out his hand and closed it.

'You know, comrades,' he said. 'I've got Hannetjie. I'll betray him tomorrow.'

Everyone began talking at once.

'Forget it, brother. You'll get shot.'

Brille laughed.

'I won't', he said. 'That is what I mean about evil. I am a father of children and I saw today that Hannetjie is just a child and stupidly truthful. I'm going to punish him severely because we need a good warder.'

The following day, with Brille as witness, Hannetjie confessed to the theft of the fertilizer and was fined a large sum of money. From then on Span One did very much as they pleased while Warder Hannetjie stood by and said nothing. But it was Brille who carried this to extremes. One day, at the close of work Warder Hannetjie said: 'Brille, pick up my jacket and carry it back to the camp.'

'But nothing in the regulations says I'm your servant, Hannetjie,' Brille replied coolly.

'I've told you not to call me Hannetjie. You must say, Baas,' but Warder Hannetjie's voice lacked conviction. In turn, Brille squinted up at him.

'I'll tell you something about this Baas business, Hannetjie,' he said. 'One of these days we are going to run the country. You are going to clean my car. Now I have a fifteen year old son and I'd die of shame if you had to tell him that I ever called you Baas.'

Warder Hannetjie went red in the face and picked up his coat.

On another occasion Brille was seen to be walking about the prison yard, openly smoking tobacco. On being taken before the prison commander he claimed to have received the tobacco from Warder Hannetjie. All throughout the tirade from his chief, Warder Hannetjie failed to defend himself but his nerve broke completely. He called Brille to one side.

'Brille,' he said. 'This thing between you and me must end. You may not know it but I have a wife and children and you're driving me to suicide.'

'Why don't you like your own medicine, Hannetjie?' Brille asked quietly.

'I can give you anything you want,' Warder Hannetjie said in desperation.

'It's not only me but the whole of Span One,' said Brille, cunningly. 'The whole of Span One wants something from you.'

Warder Hannetjie brightened with relief.

'I tink I can manage if it's tobacco you want,' he said.

Brille looked at him, for the first time struck with pity, and guilt.

He wondered if he had carried the whole business too far. The man was really a child.

'It's not tobacco we want, but you,' he said. 'We want you on our side. We want a good warder because without a good warder we won't be able to manage the long stretch ahead.'

Warder Hannetjie interpreted this request in his own fashion and his interpretation of what was good and human often left the prisoners of Span One speechless with surprise. He had a way of slipping off his revolver and picking up a spade and digging alongside Span One. He had a way of producing unheard of luxuries like boiled eggs from his farm nearby and things like cigarettes, and Span One responded nobly and got the reputation of being the best work span in the camp. And it wasn't only take from their side. They were awfully good at stealing certain commodities like fertilizer which were needed on the farm of Warder Hannetjie.

Notes

span — Afrikaans: team or squad

Brille — Afrikaans: spectacles

knobkerrie — clublike stick

Mr Drum Goes to Jail

Henry Nxumalo

We were taken to Johannesburg Central Prison by truck. We arrived at the prison immediately after one o'clock. From the truck we were given orders to 'shayisa' (close up), fall in twos and 'sharp shoot' (run) to the prison reception office. From then on 'Come on, Kaffir!' was the operative phase from both black and white prison officials, and in all languages.

Many of us who were going to prison for the first time didn't know exactly where the reception office was. Although the prison officials were with us, no one was directing us. But if a prisoner hesitated, slackened his half-running pace and looked round, he got a hard boot kick on the buttocks, a slap on his face or a whipping from the warders. Fortunately there were some second offenders with us who knew where to go. We followed them through the prison's many zig-zagging corridors until we reached the reception office.

The reception office had a terrifyingly brutal atmosphere. It was full of foul language. A number of khaki-uniformed white officials stood behind a long cement bar-like curved counter. They wore the initials 'P.S.G.D.' on their shoulders. When they were not joking about prisoners they were swearing at them and taking down their particulars. Two were taking fingerprints and hitting the prisoners in the face when they made mistakes.

Five long-term prisoners attended to us. One came up to me and said he knew me. I didn't know him. He asked for cigarettes, but I didn't have any. Another told us to take off our watches and money and hold them in our hands. These were to be kept separate from our other possessions. Another asked me for 2s. 6d.; but I had 5d. only and he wasn't interested. He noticed I had a copy of *Time* magazine in my hand and asked for it. I gave it to him. He hid it under the counter so that the warders couldn't see it. Later he asked me what paper it was, how old it was and whether it was interesting. After we had undressed, one long-term prisoner demanded my fountain pen.

'That's a fine pen you've got, eh?' he asked. 'How about giving it to me?'

I said: 'I'm afraid I can't; it's not my pen, it's my boss's pen.'

'Hi, don't tell me lies, you bastard,' he said. 'What the hell are you doing with your boss's pen in prison? Did you steal it?' he asked.

I said I hadn't stolen it. I was using it and had it in my possession when I was arrested.

'Give it here. I want it for my work here; if you refuse you'll see blood streaming down your dirty mouth soon.' I was nervous, but didn't reply.

'Look, you little fool, I'll see that you are well treated in prison if you give me that pen.'

The other prisoners looked at me anxiously. I didn't know whether they approved of my giving my pen or not; but their anxious look seemed to suggest that their fate in prison lay in that pen. I gave it away.

We were called up to have our fingerprints taken by a white warder. Before taking the impression the warder made a loud complaint that the hand glove he used when taking impressions was missing. He swore at the long-term prisoner who assisted him and told him to find it. The other white prison officials helped him find the glove. He was a stout, middle-aged man, apparently a senior official. He took my impression, examined it and then complained that my hands were wet. He hit me on the mouth with the back of his gloved hand. I rubbed my right thumb on my hair and he took another impression.

From there I ran down to the end of the wide curved desk to have my height taken, and stood beside the measuring rod, naked. A long-term prisoner took my height. When finished with a prisoner, he would throw his ticket on the floor for the prisoner to pick up.

We were then taken to the showers in another room. There was neither soap nor a towel. After a few minutes under water we were told to get out, and skip to get dry. Then our prison clothes were thrown at us — a red shirt and a torn white pair of short pants. They looked clean; but the side cap and the white jacket which were issued to me later were filthy. The jacket had dry sweat on the neck.

From then on we were barefoot, and were marched to the hospital for medical examination in double time. Another long-term prisoner lined us up, ordered us to undress and turn our faces to the wall, so that we would not pollute the medical officer with our breath when he came to examine us.

After this we were marched down to the main court of the prison in double time. Here we found different white and black warders and long-term prisoners, who took charge of us. Again we undressed and had our second shower in thirty minutes. I was unable to make out my own clothes after the shower and the skipping. The African warder kicked me in the stomach with the toe of his boot. I tried to hold the boot to protect myself, and fell on my face. He asked if I had an operation to my stomach. I said no. He looked at me scornfully. I got up, picked up the clothes in front of me and ran to join the others squatting on the floor.

After another rollcall we were marched to the top of the court to collect our food. The dishes were lined in rows and each prisoner picked up the dish nearest him. The zinc dishes containing the food were rusty. The top of my dish was broken on three places. The food itself was boiled whole mealies with fat. We were marched to No. 7 cell, given blankets and a sleeping-mat and locked in. We ate. The time was about 4.30 p.m. Clean water and toilet buckets were installed, but the water wasn't enough for sixty people. The long-term prisoners warned us not to use the water as if we were at our homes. An old man went to fetch water with his dish at one stage and the long-term prisoner in charge of the cell swore at him. The old man insisted that he was thirsty and continued scooping the water. The long-term prisoner took the water away from him and threw it all over the old man's face.

There was a stinking smell when prisoners used the toilet bucket at night without toilet paper. At 8 p.m. the bell rang and we were ordered to be quiet and sleep. Some prisoners who had smuggled *dagga* and matches into the cell started conversing in whispers, and smoking. The blankets were full of bugs; I turned round and round during the night without being able to sleep, and kept my prison clothes on for protection against bugs.

We were up at about six o'clock the following morning. I tried to get some water to wash my dish and drink. The dish was full of the previous night's fat, and I didn't know how I was going to do it. But the long-term prisoner shouted at me and ordered me to leave the water alone. I obeyed. He swore at me in Afrikaans, and ordered me to wipe the urine which was overflowing from the toilet bucket with a small sack of cloth. I did so. He said I must wipe it dry; but the cloth was so small that the floor remained wet.

He told me to find two other prisoners to help me carry the toilet bucket out, empty it and clean it. It was full of the night's excrement. There were no volunteers, so I slipped to a corner and waited. He saw me and rushed at me.

'What did I tell you, damn it, what did I say?' He slapped me on the left cheek with his open right hand as he spoke. He said he could have put me in solitary confinement if he wished. He could tell the chief warder that I had messed the floor and I would get an additional punishment. I kept quiet. I had done nothing of the sort. Finally he ordered two other prisoners to help me.

We emptied the bucket and washed it as the other prisoners were being lined up in readiness for breakfast. One of my colleagues tried to wash his hands after we had emptied the bucket. The white warder saw him and slashed him with the strap part of his baton. The dish containing my porridge — and many others — still had the previous night's fat. It had been washed in cold water. The breakfast itself was yellow porridge with half-cooked pieces of turnips, potatoes, carrots and other vegetables I could not recognise. No spoons are provided; so I had my breakfast with my stinking soiled hands. I didn't feel like eating, but feared that I would be inviting further trouble.

After breakfast we were divided into many work 'spans' (parties). I spent my first day with a span cutting grass, pulling out weeds with my hands and pushing wheelbarrows at the Johannesburg Teachers' Training College in Parktown. We walked for about half a mile to our place of work, and I was one of two prisoners carrying a heavy, steel food can, which contained lunch porridge for a party of sixteen. Two warders escorted us: one white and one black. Once I slackened because we were going down a precipice: my fingers were sore and the burden was heavy. The old white warder who was carrying a big rifle slashed me on my bare legs with the strap of his baton.

We returned to jail at four. We were ordered to undress and 'tausa,' a common routine of undressing prisoners when they return from work, searching their clothes, their mouths, armpits, and rectum for hidden articles. I didn't know how it was done. I opened my mouth, turned round and didn't jump and clap my hands. The white warder conducting the search hit me with his fist on my left jaw, threw my clothes at me and went on searching the others. I ran off, and joined the food queue.

One night I didn't have a mat to sleep on. Long-term prisoners in charge of the cells sometimes took a bundle of mats to make themselves comfortable beds, to the discomfort of other prisoners. In practice, a prisoner never knows where he will sleep next day. It is all determined by your speed in 'tausa', food and blanket queues. A prisoner uses another prisoner's dirty blankets every night.

In the four days I was in prison — I got a remission of one day — I was kicked or thrashed every day. I saw many other prisoners being thrashed daily. I was never told what was expected of me, but had to guess. Sometimes I guessed wrong and got into trouble.

Long-term and short-term prisoners mixed freely in the prison. For example, the famous Tiger, of Alexandra township, who was doing a ten-year sentence for various crimes, was one of the most important persons in prison during my time. He was responsible for the in and out movements of other prisoners and warders. Though I

174

was a short-term prisoner, I too, took orders from Tiger.

It was a common practice for short-term prisoners to give their small piece of meat to long-term prisoners on meat days for small favours such as tobacco, *dagga*, shoes (which are supposed to be supplied to Coloured prisoners only), wooden spoons − or to ensure that they were always supplied with sleeping-mats.

Thrashing time for warders was roll call, breakfast time and supper time. For long-term prisoners it was inside the cells at all times. Long-term prisoners thrashed prisoners more severely and more often than the prison officials themselves, and often in the presence of either white or black warders.

On the day of our discharge we were marched to the reception office for our personal effects and checking out. The long-term prisoners officiating there told us not to think that we were already out of prison. They kicked and slapped prisoners for the slightest mistake, and sometimes for no mistake at all; and promised them additional sentences if they complained. In the office there was a notice warning prisoners to see that their personal belongings were recorded in the prison's book correctly, and exactly as they had brought them. But I dared not complain about my pen which was commandeered on my arrival, lest I be detained. The prisoner who took it pretended not to know me.

Before we left the prison we were told the superintendent would address us. We could make complaints to him if we had any. But the fat Zulu warder who paraded us to the yard for the superintendent's inspection said we must tell him everything was all right if we wanted to leave prison.

'This is a court of law,' he said; 'you are about to go home, but before you leave this prison the big boss of the prison will address you. He will ask you if you have any complaints. Now I take it that you all want to go to your homes − to your wives and children − you don't want to stay here. So if the big boss asks you if everything is all right, say: "Yes, sir." If he says have you any complaints say: "No, sir." You hear?'

In a chorus we said 'Yes.'

Just then one prisoner complained that his Kliptown train ticket was missing from his things. It was a season ticket. The Zulu warder pulled him aside and said:

'You think you're clever, eh? You'll see!' He put him at the tail-end of the parade. The superintendent came and we answered him as instructed. Most of us were seeing him for the first time. The Zulu warder said nothing about the complaint of the man from Kliptown. Later, as we were going to collect our monies from the pay office, the man from Kliptown was escorted to the reception office to see C., the famous fierce discharge officer. C. said the man's papers showed that he was discharged at Fordsburg and not at Kliptown. He was not entitled to any ticket. But the man insisted that he was arrested at Kliptown, charged at Fordsburg and appeared in Johannesburg. The fat Zulu warder said in broken Afrikaans: 'He's mad, sir.'

He gave the man a hard slap in the face with his open hand, and said:

'You're just wasting the boss's time, eh? On your way . . . voetsak!' And the man sneaked out.

One by one we zig-zagged our way out of the prison's many doors and gates and lined up in twos in front of the main and final gate. We were ordered to leave prison quietly and in pairs when the small gate was open. If we blocked the gate we would be thrashed. We were to come out in the order of the line. The man on the left would go out first and the one on the right would follow. The gate was opened. We saw freedom and blocked the gate in our anxiety. If they thrashed us we couldn't feel it . . . we didn't look back!

Notes

PSDG — Prisons Service Gevangenis Diens

voetsak, or voetsek — 'a rough command to be off, go away, usually to a dog; offensive when applied to a person' (Branford Dictionary)

Many South Africans have been subject to the state legislation which allows detention without charge or trial. Such detention, often without legal representation or family visits and in solitary confinement, causes dreadful unhappiness and anxiety (a Detainees' Parents Support Committee, formed to help, has effectively been banned by Government Emergency Regulations in early 1988), and sometimes tragedy results. More than sixty people have died in detention — in 1977 Steve Biko was the forty-sixth. There is scepticism about some of the official reasons given for these deaths. For instance, Ahmed Timol (d 1971) 'fell from a tenth floor window' at Johannesburg security Police headquarters, Imam Abdullah Haron (d 1969) 'slipped down the stairs', no explanation being given for the twenty-seven bruises found on his body, and Solomon Modipane (d 1969) 'slipped on a piece of soap and fatally injured himself'.

Possibilities for a Man Hunted by SBs

Farouk Asvat

> There's one of two possibilities
> Either they find you or they don't
> If they don't it's ok
> But if they find you
> There's one of two possibilities
> Either they let you go or they ban you
> If they let you go it's ok
> But if they ban you
> There's one of two possibilities
> Either you break your ban or you don't
> If you don't it's ok
> But if you break your ban
> There's one of two possibilities
> Either they find out or they don't
> If they don't it's ok
> But if they find out
> There's one of two possibilities
> Either they find you guilty or notguilty
> If they find you notguilty it's ok
> But if they find you guilty
> There's one of two possibilities
> Either they suspend your sentence or they jail you
> If they suspend your sentence it's ok
> But if they jail you
> There's one of two possibilities
> Either they release you
> Or you fall from the tenth floor

Notes
SBs — the Special (Political) Branch of the South African Police

In Detention

Chris van Wyk

He fell from the ninth floor
He hanged himself
He slipped on a piece of soap while washing
He hanged himself
He slipped on a piece of soap while washing
He fell from the ninth floor
He hanged himself while washing
He slipped from the ninth floor
He hung from the ninth floor
He slipped on the ninth floor while washing
He fell from a piece of soap while slipping
He hung from the ninth floor
He washed from the ninth floor while slipping
He hung from a piece of soap while washing

Detention

Achmat Dangor

They came
with the usual fanfare,
screeching brakes
and the crash of doors,
and took you away,
flimsily dressed.

I watched
the fragile warmth
of our lovemaking,
wrapped around you
like a bright coat,
dissipate in the cold air,
I had nothing to offer
but silence.

I will search for you
in the labyrinth corridors
that are to become
the days of our life,
and search for your eyes
behind the blur
of barred windows,
I will whisper
too softly
in the clamour
of visiting rooms

I could put you
in one of my poems,
as a last resort.

Points for Discussion

● Dennis Brutus's sequence of poems called LETTERS TO MARTHA is
the work of a fine mind and an acute sensitivity. These poems must rank
among the most telling in all prison literature. Can you pinpoint particular
reasons for this?

● WALKING ON AIR is an amazingly moving poem. Try to analyse why
this is so. Is it because John Matthews is such an unassuming, ordinary
person? Is it because his wife Dulcie (who 'isn't political at all', remember)
is so immediately understanding and loyal? How strongly — and yet with
what spareness — Cronin builds their love! And what admiration he feels
for Matthews!

● THE PRISONER WHO WORE GLASSES is a wry little story of how
the intention of political imprisonment can be subverted if you're wily and
shrewd enough — and play the game by its own rules. How much respect
do you feel for Brille? and how much for the Hannetjie of the last few
paragraphs of the story?

● Where do the interest and excitement lie in the kind of newspaper-
reporting that Henry Nxumalo became famous for in *Drum* magazine?
Clearly, you can assume that nothing the reporter is writing is fictional —
is that part of it?

● The first two poems about detention (by Farouk Asvat and Chris van
Wyk) are grimly funny. What's your response to these pieces of macabre
humour (often called 'black comedy', but that's a confusing term to use in
Southern Africa!)? How does the humour work? What's its purpose or
intention? Remember that most comedy — even the genteelest, such as

Jane Austen's — offers a serious critical commentary on the writer's society.

● On quite the other hand, the section ends with a very delicate poem by Dangor. Do you prefer this sort of response and treatment?

Ourselves again

To finish with positive and exuberant words of strength, read Mongane Serote from *There Will be a Better Time*

from **There Will be a Better Time**

Mongane Serote

. . .
time has run out for those who ride on others
if the we is the most of us
and the most of us is the will
the will to say no!
when the most of us will create a better time
there will be a better time
when time has run out for liars
for those who take and take and take from others, take
    forever!
and keep taking
for themselves alone
take and take and take
time has run out
when we say no!
no more —
— no more is not a word but an act, remember that —
my little friend
no more starts with learning to learn
learn to carry the past
like we do with dirty clothes
carry them to the washing place and wash them
we carry the past to the present

181

and wash it by learning what it means
when what it means becomes our action
because we have learnt it
like you learn two plus two is four
so you can count four if you have four sweets
we use the past we learnt like that
we say grandma and grandpa and pa and ma come from here
we are born here, so we are here
here is our land.

. . .

no we say
no we say in one voice
no more we say
no more of the bad time.
the past is here now
the present sings the solos of our warriors
it sings it in a choir of our voices
like a strong wind a hurricane
the present sings our song from the past
like a mad storm
no!
no one will have plenty when we have nothing
this is a big land as big as the sky
we can live here
we say
all of us can have enough from this land
we say like our warriors said
from a long time past
this is our land
we say
we will live like this is our land
we say
like our warriors said
and time knows them like we know them
no they said
and we say no!
yes there will be a better time because we say so
there will be a better time because like our warriors
we make a better time and many of us know that we can
     and must
there will be a better time
we say

time has run our for our bad time
we say we learnt from bad times to make time better —
like a boiling pot spills water
our country spills us now
we ask for sleeping space in foreign lands
sleep sleepless nights in prison
die like dogs thrown away in the streets
spill our blood like dirty water
so it seems my little friend, so it seems
here is a better time
we learn
from the knowledge of the world
that we have to know what we want
and what cannot be wanted by anyone
and from the dark of the past we create a better time
bright like a brand new day
a day we make
a better time
ah
there *will* be a better time made by us.

About Contributors

Farouk Asvat   Born 1952 in Johannesburg. A five-year banning order was served on him from 1973 to 1978. In 1978 he qualified as a medical doctor. He now works in Johannesburg in social and community health, as well as being a part-time journalist.

Published works

Poetry
The Time of Our Lives, Black Thoughts Publications 1982
A Celebration of Flames, Ad. Donker 1987, (winner of the AA mutual
   Poetry Award)

Dennis Brutus   Guy Butler

Dennis Brutus   Born 1924 in Harare, Zimbabwe (then Salisbury, Rhodesia). He spent his childhood in Dowarville township in Port Elizabeth. He graduated from Fort Hare University College, taught for 14 years and campaigned against racism in sport. In 1963 he was arrested, released and banned. He fled to Swaziland, but was not granted a residence permit there; on his way to an Olympic meeting in Germany he was detained at Maputo (then Lourenco Marques) and handed over to the South African police. He attempted to escape, was shot, and sentenced to 18 months' hard labour on Robben Island. In 1965 he was released, and immediately had a new banning order served on him. In 1966 he left South Africa on an exit permit. He has been active in the International Defence and Aid Fund, and as the President of SANROC (the South African Non Racial Open Committee of Olympic Sports). In 1970 he addressed the United Nations Special Committee on Apartheid. He is now Professor of English Literature at Northwestern University in Chicago. He was awarded the Mbari Poetry Prize in 1962 for his first collection of poems; he rejected the award as discriminatory in that only black poets were eligible.

Published works:

Poetry
Sirens, Knuckles and Bones, Mbari Publications 1963
Letters to Martha, Heinemann African Writers Series 1968
Climates of Love and Continents, in *Seven South African Poets* ed. Cosmo
    Pieterse, Heinemann African Writers Series 1971
A Simple Lust, Heinemann African Writers Series 1973.
A Stubborn Hope, Heinemann African Writers Series 1978.

Guy Butler   Born 1918 in Cradock in the Eastern Cape. After spending his boyhood there, he was a student at Rhodes University, and was awarded the Queen Victoria Scholarship to Oxford. He served in the South African army for 5 years (in the Middle East and Italy). After the war he went to Brasenose College, Oxford. He then briefly lectured at the University of the Witwatersrand. He has had a long and distinguished career as Professor of English at Rhodes University, where he was Head of the Department from 1952 to 1980. He was awarded the CNA Literary Award in 1975 for his *Selected Poems*.

Published works:

Poetry
Stranger to Europe, Balkema 1952, with additional poems 1960
South of The Zambesi, Abelard-Schuman 1966
On First Seeing Florence, New Coin 1968
Selected Poems, Ad. Donker 1975
Songs and Ballads, David Philip 1978
Pilgrimage to Diaz Cross, David Philip 1988

185

Plays
The Dam, Balkema 1953
The Dove Returns, Fortune Press & Balkema 1956
Cape Charade, Balkema 1968
Take Root or Die, Balkema 1970
Richard Gosh of Salem, Maskew Miller 1982
Edited
A Book of South African Verse, Oxford University Press, 1959
(with Chris Mann) *A New Book of South African Verse In English*, Oxford
University Press 1979
When Boys Were Men, Oxford University Press 1969
The 1820 Settlers, Human & Rousseau 1974
Autobiography
Karoo Morning, David Philip 1977
Bursting World, David Philip 1983
Book in his honour
ed. Malvern van Wyk Smith & Don Maclennan *Olive Schreiner and After:
Essays on Southern African Literature, in Honour of Guy Butler*, David
Philip 1983

Jeni Couzyn   Born 1942 in Johannesburg. She studied at the University of
Natal. She taught for the African Music and Drama Association in Soweto.
In 1965 she moved to the United Kingdom. Her work has been read at
universities, arts festivals, on radio and television. She became the Chair-
person of the National Poetry Secretariat in 1973. She has recently lived and
taught at the University of Victoria, British Columbia, Canada. She now
lives in London.

Published works

Poetry
Flying, Workshop Press 1970
Monkey's Wedding, Jonathan Cape 1972
Christmas in Africa, Heinemann 1975
Life by Drowning 1983

Jeremy Cronin   Born 1949 in Cape Town, the son of an officer in the
South African Navy, he spent most of his childhood in various naval bases,
especially Simon's Town. After the death of his father, he moved to
Rondebosch, where he went to St Joseph's Marist Brothers College. He
studied at the University of Cape Town and in Paris. He returned to Cape
Town in 1974 and lectured in the Philosophy and Politics Departments. He
was arrested in 1976 and charged under the Terrorism Act for having
carried out ANC underground work for several years. He spent most of his

Jeni Couzyn

Jeremy Cronin

sentence in various security prisons in Pretoria, including three years among death row prisoners in the Pretoria Maximum Security prison. During his sentence his wife unexpectedly died. Cronin was released from jail in May 1983. He is again on the staff of the University of Cape Town. His collection of poems won him the Ingrid Jonker Prize for poetry in 1984.

Published works

Poetry
Inside, Ravan Press 1984

Achmat Dangor   Born 1948 in Johannesburg. Between 1973 and 1978 he was a banned person in South Africa. In 1980 he won the Mofolo-Plomer Prize for his collection of short stories, including the brilliant novella *Waiting For Leila*. He is now a manager for an international company in Johannesburg.

Published works

Poetry
Bulldozer, Ravan Press 1983

187

Achmat Dangor   Ahmed Essop

Short Stories
Waiting For Leila and Other Stories, Ravan Press 1981
Edited
(with Michael Chapman), *Voices From Within*, Ad. Donker 1982

Modikwe Dikobe   Born 1913 in Seabe in the Northern Transvaal. At the age of 10 he went to Johannesburg, living in Sophiatown and Doornfontein. He left school after Std 6. He has worked as a newspaper-seller, a hawker, a clerk, a bookkeeper, a trade unionist and a nightwatchman. He took his Junior Certificate by correspondence. In 1977 he retired to a small plot in what is now part of Bophuthatswana.

Published works

Poetry
Dispossessed, Ravan Press 1983
Novels
The Marabi Dance, Heinemann African Writers Series 1973

Ahmed Essop   Born 1931 in India. With a BA Honours in English from the University of South Africa, he has taught in various schools in Fordsburg and Lenasia. In 1979 he won the Olive Schreiner Prize, awarded by the English Academy of Southern Africa, for his short stories.

Published works

Novels
The Visitation, Ravan Press 1980
The Emperor, Ravan Press 1984
Short Stories
The Hajji and Other Stories, Ravan Press 1978

Nadine Gordimer   Born 1923 in what was then the small mining town of Springs, where she attended a convent school. She studied at and graduated from the University of the Witwatersrand. She is South Africa's most distinguished and honoured novelist and short story writer. Her work has on occasion been banned in South Africa and then been unbanned. She has always lived in South Africa, rejecting exile: 'One must look at the world *from Africa*, to be an African writer, not look *upon* Africa from the world.' In another context she says, 'In South Africa the reader knows perilously little about himslf or his feelings. We have a great deal to learn about ourselves, and the novelist, along with the poet, playwright, composer and painter, must teach us.' Among the literary prizes Nadine Gordimer has won are: the CNA Prize (3 times), the Booker McConnell Prize 1974, the W H Smith Award 1960, the James Tait Black Memorial Prize 1972, the Modern Languages Association International Award 1981, the French award the Grand Aigle d'Or. In 1981 she was awarded the Scottish Arts Council's Neil Gunn Followship. She has been Visiting Professor at Columbia University.

Published works

Novels
The Lying Days, Victor Gollanz 1953, Virago press 1983
A World of Strangers, Victor Gollanz 1958, Simon & Shuster 1958, Penguin 1962, Jonathan Cape 1976
Occasion for Loving, Victor Gollanz 1963, Virago Press 1983
The Late Bourgeois World, Jonathan Cape 1966, **Viking Press 1966**, Macmillan 1966, Penguin 1982
A Guest of Honour, Viking Press 1970, Jonathan Cape 1971, Penguin 1973
The Observationist, Jonathan Cape 1974, Penguin 1976
Burger's Daughter, Jonathan Cape 1979, Viking Press 1979, Penguin 1980
July's People, Ravan Press & Taurus 1981, Jonathan Cape 1981, Penguin 1982
A Sport of Nature, David Philip 1987

Short Stories

Face to Face, Silver Leaf Books 1949
The Soft Voice of the Serpent, Victor Gollanz 1953
Six Feet of the Country, Victor Gollanz 1956, Penguin 1982
Friday's Footprint, Victor Gollanz 1960
Not for Publication, Victor Gollanz 1965
Livingstone's Companions, Jonathan Cape 1972, Penguin 1975
Selected Stories, Jonathan Cape 1976, Penguin 1980
Some Monday for Sure, Heinemann African Writers Series 1976
A Soldier's Embrace Viking Press 1980, Penguin 1982
Something Out There Ravan Press & Taurus 1984, Jonathan Cape 1984

Critical writing

The Black Interpreters, Spro-cas Ravan 1973
What Happened to Burger's Daughter: How South African Censorship Works, Taurus 1980

Books about Nadine Gordimer

Michael Wade *Nadine Gordimer*, Modern African Writers Series Evan Brothers 1978
Stephen R Clingman *The Novels of Nadine Gordimer: History From Within* Ravan Press 1986

Nadine Gordimer   Mafika Gwala

Xolile Guma   After taking his 'A'-levels at Waterford Kamhlaba in Swaziland, he did a BA degree in Economics at the then University of Botswana, Lesotho and Swaziland, followed by an MA at the University of Toronto. He is now a Senior Lecturer in Economics in the Faculty of Social Science at the University of Swaziland. He is married to Lindiwe Sisulu, daughter of Walter Sisulu, the imprisoned ANC leader, and Albertina Sisulu.

Published works

Short Stories
'African trombone' in *Forced Landing*, Ravan Press 1979

Mafika Gwala   Born 1946 in Verulam, Natal, and matriculated at Vryheid. He has worked as a legal clerk, a factory hand, a teacher and a publications researcher. He is a founder member of the Mpumalanga Arts Ensemble. He works as an industrial relations programme officer.

Published works

Poetry
Jol' Iinkomo, Ad. Donker 1977
No More Lullabies, Ravan Press 1982

Bessie Head   (1937–1986) Born in Pietermaritzburg, brought up in various institutions in Durban. After a very difficult childhood and adolescence, she worked as a journalist (on *Drum*) and a teacher. She left South Africa on an exit permit in 1963, and she and her son settled in Botswana. She remained in exile in Serowe village, working as a teacher and a gardener until her death.

Published works

Novels
Where Rain Clouds Gather, Victor Gollanz 1968, Heinemann New Windmill
   Series 1968
Maru, Victor Gollanz 1971, Heinemann African Writers Series 1972
A Question of Power, Davis Poynter 1974, Heinemann African Writers
   Series 1974
Short Stories
The Collector of Treasures, Heinemann African Writers Series 1977, David
   Philip 1977

History, social life and customs
Serowe: Village of the Rain Wind, Heinemann African Writers Series 1981
A Bewitched Crossroad Ad. Donker 1984

Fhazel Johennesse Born 1956 in Johannesburg. He was the co-editor with
Chris van Wyk of the influential but short-lived literary journal *Wietie* in
1980, and a co-director of Sable Books. He works in the computer industry
in Johannesburg, and is married, with two children. He says: 'I have been
told that writing poetry about being black is "troublemaking". But this is so
wrong. My writing is a confirmation of my humanity, a celebration of my
blackness.'

Published works

Poetry
The Rainmaker, Ravan Press 1979

Mike Kirkwood Born 1943 in St Vincent, West Indies. After teaching in
the English Department of the University of Natal and being Editor of the
literary journal *Bolt* for some years, he became the Director of Ravan
Press, and launched many new writers, as well as starting *Staffrider* magazine.
He now lives in the United Kingdom.

Published works

Poetry
Between Islands, Beteleur Press 1975

Alex la Guma (1925–1985) Born in Cape Town, he was educated at
Trafalgar High School and the Cape Technical College. He worked as a
clerk, factory-hand, bookkeeper and journalist. He was a member of the
South African Communist Party until it was banned in 1950; he helped to
organize both the Kliptown Conference in 1955 and the formulation of the
Freedom Charter. Between 1956 and 1960 he was one of the 156 accused in
the Treason Trial. In the 1960 State of Emergency he was detained for 5
months; in 1962 he was banned and placed under house arrest for 5 years;
during this time he was again detained under the 90-day and later the 180-
day regulations. In 1966 he left South Africa, lived in the United Kingdom
for some years, and then settled in Cuba, where he was the ANC's Chief
Representative for the Caribbean and Latin America until his death. In
1969 he was awarded the Afro-Asian Prize for Literature. His novels and
short stories have earned him a secure place as one of South Africa's
foremost writers.

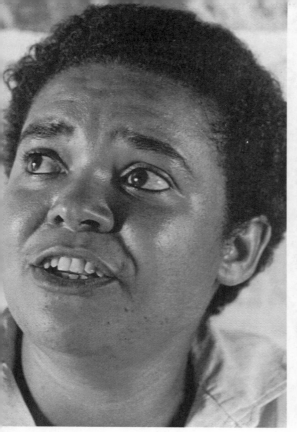

Bessie Head

Mike Kirkwood

Chris van Wyk and Fhazel Johennesse

Alex la Guma

Douglas Livingstone

Published works

Novella
A Walk in the Night, Mbari Publications 1962, Heinemann African Writers
Series 1968, Northwestern University Press 1967
Novels
And a Threefold Cord, Seven Seas Books 1964
The Stone Country, Seven Seas Books 1967, Heinemann African Writers
Series 1974
In the Fog of the Season's End, Heinemann African Writers Series 1972
Time of the Butcherbird, Heinemann African Writers Series 1979
Short Stories
in *Quartet* ed. Richard Rive, Heinemann African Writers Series 1965

Douglas Livingstone   Born 1932 in Kuala Lumpur, Malaya. After living
through the Japanese invasion of Malaya, Livingstone's family settled in
Natal. He went to school in Margate and Port Shepstone, and then to
Kearsney College. He qualified as a bacteriologist in 1958 in Zimbabwe
(then Southern Rhodesia), and worked in Zambia (then Northern Rhodesia).
In 1964 he moved to Durban, where he has been in charge of marine

bacteriological research for a South African water-research institute. He is one of South Africa's most highly regarded poets, his work being known and published internationally. In 1965 he won the Guinness Poetry Prize, in 1970 the Cholmondley Award, in 1975 the Olive Schreiner Prize for his play *A Rhino for the Boardroom* in 1977 the South African English Association Prize, and in 1985 the CNA Prize for his *Selected Poems*.

Published works (excluding his scientific publications)

Poetry
The Skull in the Mud, Outposts Publications 1960
Sjambok and Other Poems from Africa, Oxford University Press 1964
(with Thomas Kinsella & Anne Sexton) *Poems*, Oxford University Press 1968
Eyes Closed Against the Sun, Oxford University Press 1970
The Anvil's Undertone, Ad. Donker 1978
A Rosary of Bone David Philip 1975
A Rosary of Bone, Second Edition, with more poems, David Philip 1983
Selected Poems, Ad. Donker 1985
Plays
A Rhino for the Boardroom in *Contemporary South African Plays*, ed. Ernest Pereira, Ravan Press 1977
The Sea My Winding-sheet in *Theatre One* ed. Stephen Gray Ad. Donker 1978
Critical article
Douglas Livingstone, 'The poetry of Mtshali, Serote, Sepanla and others in English: Notes towards a Critical Evaluation' in *New Classic* No 3, 1976
Book about Douglas Livingstone
Michael Chapman. *Douglas Livingstone: A Critical Study of his Poetry*, Ad. Donker 1981

Matsemela Manaka   Born 1956. He is a musician and a graphic artist (he has had exhibitions in Europe) as well as a playwright. He has had a number of plays performed at the Market Theatre, Johannesburg, in the United Kingdom and in Europe. In *Egoli*, he acknowledges the contribution of the two actors, John Moalusi Ledwaba and Hamilton Silwane.

Published works

Plays
Egoli, Ravan Press 1980
Rula in *Market Plays*, ed. Stephen Gray, Ad. Donker 1986
Art
Echoes of African Art, Skotaville 1987

Chris Zithulele Mann Born 1948 in Port Elizabeth. He studied at the University of the Witwatersrand; while he was a Rhodes Scholar at Oxford he won the Newdigate Prize for poetry; he then took an MA in African Studies at the School of African and Oriental Studies at London University. He lived and taught in Swaziland, and was then on the staff of the English Department of Rhodes University. He now works for the Valley Trust, a medical and agricultural rural development scheme in Natal. He won the Olive Schreiner Prize in 1983 for his second collection of poems.

Published works

Poetry
First Poems, Bateleur Press 1977
New Shades, David Philip 1982
Edited
(with Guy Butler), *The New Book of South African Verse in English*, Oxford University Press 1979

Mtutuzeli Matshoba Born 1950 in Orlando East; brought up and still lives in Mzimhlophe in Soweto. After high school in Lovedale in the Cape and Vryheid in Natal, he went to Fort Hare until the 1976 disturbances. His brother Diliza was imprisoned on Robben Island. In 1981 he was winner of the Thomas Pringle Award given by the English Academy of Southern Africa for his collection of short stories. Of his work Matshoba says:

> I want to reflect through my works life on my side of the fence, the black side: so that whatever may happen in the future, I may not be set down as 'a bloodthirsty terrorist'. So that I may say: 'These were the events which shaped the Steve Bikos and the Solomon Mahlangus, and the many others who came before and after them.'

Published works

Short Stories
Call Me Not a Man, Ravan Press 1979, (Banned in South Africa)
Play
Seeds of War, Ravan Press 1981

Casey Motsisi (1932–1977) He was born in Western Native Township. Together with Stan Motjuwadi (present Editor of *Drum*) he attended Madibane High School and the Pretoria Normal College. Known as 'the Kid', he was one of the younger *Drum* writers, junior to Can Themba and Es'kia Mphahlele. Although he is best known as the great exponent of 'shebeen-pieces', Motsisi's range also included some poems and short stories.

Chris Zithulele Mann

Casey Motsisi

Published works

Short stories and pieces
ed Mothobi Mutloatse *Casey & Co*, Ravan Press 1978

Mbuyiseni Oswald Mtshali   Born 1940 in Vryheid, Natal. At the age of eighteen he moved to Johannesburg and had various jobs, such as being an office messenger. In 1974 he won the Olive Schreiner Prize for his first collection of poems, *Sounds of a Cowhide Drum*, which has achieved the highest sale of any book of poems published in South Africa. He studied at Columbia University; worked as an arts critic on *The Star*; was Senior Master at the Pace College in Jabulani, Soweto; and is now studying in the United States.

Published works

Poetry
Sounds of a Cowhide Drum, Renoster Books 1971, Oxford University Press
   1971, Okpaku 1972, Ad. Donker 1982
Fire Flames, Shuter & Shooter 1980

Edited
Give Us a Break, Diaries of a group of Soweto children, Skotaville 1988

Charles Mungoshi Born 1947 in Manyene near Chivhu, Zimbabwe. He was educated at All Saints School, Daramombe School and St Augustine's Secondary School. He has worked for the Forestry Commission as a research assistant; as a clerk in a bookshop; as an editor at the Literature Bureau. Some of his works were banned in Rhodesia, but have now been printed in Zimbabwe. He has won several awards, including PEN awards in 1976 and 1981. He was a literary director of Zimbabwe Publishing House for some time; and is now writer-in-residence at the University of Zimbabwe.

Published works

Poetry
The Milkman Doesn't Only Deliver Milk, Mopani Series, Poetry Society of
   Zimbabwe
Novels
Waiting for the Rain, Heinemann African Writers Series 1975, Zimbabwe
   Publishing House 1981
Short Stories
Coming of the Dry Season, Oxford University Press 1972, Zimbabwe
   Publishing House 1981
Some Kinds of Wounds and other Short Stories Mambo Press 1980

Mbuyiseni Oswald Mtshali   Mbulelo Mzamane

Chris Zithulele Mann   Casey Motsisi

Published works

Short stories and pieces
ed Mothobi Mutloatse *Casey & Co*, Ravan Press 1978

Mbuyiseni Oswald Mtshali   Born 1940 in Vryheid, Natal. At the age of
eighteen he moved to Johannesburg and had various jobs, such as being an
office messenger. In 1974 he won the Olive Schreiner Prize for his first
collection of poems, *Sounds of a Cowhide Drum*, which has achieved the
highest sale of any book of poems published in South Africa. He studied at
Columbia University; worked as an arts critic on *The Star*; was Senior
Master at the Pace College in Jabulani, Soweto; and is now studying in the
United States.

Published works

Poetry
Sounds of a Cowhide Drum, Renoster Books 1971, Oxford University Press
   1971, Okpaku 1972, Ad. Donker 1982
Fire Flames, Shuter & Shooter 1980

Edited
Give Us a Break, Diaries of a group of Soweto children, Skotaville 1988

Charles Mungoshi   Born 1947 in Manyene near Chivhu, Zimbabwe. He was educated at All Saints School, Daramombe School and St Augustine's Secondary School. He has worked for the Forestry Commission as a research assistant; as a clerk in a bookshop; as an editor at the Literature Bureau. Some of his works were banned in Rhodesia, but have now been printed in Zimbabwe. He has won several awards, including PEN awards in 1976 and 1981. He was a literary director of Zimbabwe Publishing House for some time; and is now writer-in-residence at the University of Zimbabwe.

Published works

Poetry
The Milkman Doesn't Only Deliver Milk, Mopani Series, Poetry Society of
   Zimbabwe
Novels
Waiting for the Rain, Heinemann African Writers Series 1975, Zimbabwe
   Publishing House 1981
Short Stories
Coming of the Dry Season, Oxford University Press 1972, Zimbabwe
   Publishing House 1981
Some Kinds of Wounds and other Short Stories Mambo Press 1980

Mbuyiseni Oswald Mtshali   Mbulelo Mzamane

Mbulelo Mzamane   Born 1948 in Brakpan. He matriculated at St Christopher's High School, and obtained an MA in English Literature at what was then the University of Botswana, Lesotho and Swaziland. He taught literature at the University of Botswana. He studied at the University of Sheffield, and was awarded a PhD. He teaches at the University of Botswana. In 1966 he won the Mofolo-Plomer Literary Prize. He is known as a novelist, short story writer and literary commentator.

Published works

Novel
Children of Soweto Ravan Press 1982
Short Stories
Mzala, Ravan Press 1980
also published as *My Cousin Comes to Jo'burg*, Longmans 1981
Edited
Selected Poems of Mongane Serote, Ad. Donker 1982
Selected Poems of Sipho Sepamla, Ad. Donker 1984

Motshile Nthodi   Born 1948 in Lady Selborn Township, Pretoria. He went to school in Pretoria, while living in Mamelodi. He is a graphic artist who has exhibited and sold his work internationally. In the late 1970s he won a scholarship to study fine arts in Paris.

Published works

Poetry
From The Calabash, Ravan Press 1978

Henry Nxumalo   (1918–1957) He was born in Port Shepstone. He went to school at St Francis, Mariannhill, but had to leave while he was doing his Matric, as his father died and he needed to support the other six children in the family. He worked for a while as a domestic servant in Durban, then as a messenger and 'office-boy' for the *Bantu World* in Johannesburg: three years later he was the newspaper's sports editor. He served as a sergeant up north during World War Two; returned to *Bantu World*; then in 1951 he joined *Drum*. Known as 'Mr Drum', he pioneered what has come to be termed 'investigative reporting' in South African journalism. In order to report on conditions on the labour-farms around Bethal, he went and lived and worked on one. Having received reports of ill-treatment in South African prisons, he contrived to have himself arrested. He was found stabbed to death in a street in Western Township (now a part of Soweto).

Article
quoted in Anthony Sampson, *Drum*, Hodder & Stoughton 1956, 1983.

Henry Nxumalo   Alan Paton

Alan Paton   Born 1903 in Pietermaritzburg. He was educated at Maritzburg
College and the University of Natal (with a BSc degree). After 3 years as a
teacher at Ixopo, he was the Principal of the Diepkloof Reformatory for 13
years. He was responsible for some strikingly progressive changes in the
running of the institution, and his work there had an influence on international
penal education for the young. From 1948 he has had a most distinguished
international career in literature, and has been awarded numerous prizes
and honorary degrees and doctorates from Yale, Kenyon, Harvard, Rhodes,
Natal, Trent and Edinburgh Universities. He was the founder and National
Chairman of the South African Liberal Party until it was disbanded in 1968
as new legislation prevented its having a multi-racial membership. In 1960
he received the Freedom House Award of the United States of America; on
returning from New York his passport was withdrawn. He died in April
1988.

Published Works

Poetry and short pieces
Knocking on the Door, David Philip 1975

200

Novels
Cry the Beloved Country, Charles Scribner's Sons 1948, Jonathan Cape 1948, Penguin 1958
Too Late the Phalarope, Jonathan Cape 1955, Penguin 1971
Ah, But Your Land is Beautiful, David Philip 1981, Penguin 1982

Short Stories
Debbie Go Home, Jonathan Cape 1961, Penguin 1965

Play
(with Krishna Shah), *Sponono*, Charles Scribner's Sons 1965, David Philip 1983

Biography
Hofmeyr, Jonathan Cape 1964
also published as
South African Tragedy: The Life and Times of Jan Hofmeyr, Charles Scribner's Sons 1965
Apartheid and the Archbishop, David Philip 1973

Autobiography
Kontakion for you Departed, Jonathan Cape 1969
Towards the Mountain, David Philip 1980, OUP 1981.
Diepkloof, ed. Clyde Broster. David Philip 1986

Religious
Instrument of Thy Peace, Fontana 1969.

Dan Pillay   Born 1965 in Durban. He attended school at Waterford Kamhlaba United World College of Southern Africa in Swaziland. He was a student at the University of Natal, Durban. After his Honours degree, he was then awarded a Fulbright scholarship to do his Masters degree in English in the United States.

Published works

Short Stories
'Tuesday morning in the city' in *English Alive* 1983 (SACEE)

Richard Rive   Born 1931 in District Six in Cape Town. He was at school at Trafalgar High School. He holds Bachelor degrees in English and Education from the University of Cape Town; a Master's degree from Columbia University: and a Doctorate from Oxford University for his thesis on Olive Schreiner. He spans the whole of South African literature from the mid

Dan Pillay

Sheila Roberts

Richard Rive

1950s to the present; his short stories are among those South African stories most anthologised in overseas collections and have been translated into many languages. He is the Head of the English Department at Hewat Teacher's Training College in Cape Town.

Published works

Novels
Emergency, Faber & Faber 1964, Macmillan 1970, Panafrica Library Nelson 1982, David Philip 1988
'Buckingham Palace', District Six David Philip 1986, Heinemann African Writers Series 1987
Short Stories
African Songs, Seven Seas Books 1963
in *Quartet*, Crown 1963, Heinemann African Writers Series 1965
Advance, Retreat: Selected Short Stories, David Philip 1983
Stories, Essays & Plays
Selected Writings, Ad. Donker 1977
Edited
Quartet, Crown 1963, Heinemann African Writers Series 1965
Modern African Prose, Heinemann African Writers Series 1964
Olive Shreiner: Letters 1871–1899, David Philip 1987
Autobiography
Writing Black, David Philip 1981

Sheila Roberts   Born 1937 in Johannesburg, brought up in Mayfair and educated in Potchefstroom. She later studied at the University of South Africa (an MA degree) and at Pretoria University (a PhD). For a while she was Literary Adviser for the Drama Company of the Performing Arts Council of the Transvaal. She then taught in the English Department of Pretoria University. In 1976 she won the Olive Schreiner Prize for her first collection of short stories. She is now Associate Professor of English at Michigan State University.

Published works

Poetry
Lou's Life, Bateleur Press 1977
Dialogues and Divertimenti, Ad. Donker 1985
Short Stories
Outside Life's Feast, Ad. Donker 1975
This Time of Year, Ad. Donker 1983
Novels
He's My Brother, Ad. Donker 1977
The Weekenders, Bateleur Press 1980

Sipho Sepamla Born 1932 in Krugersdorp. He trained as a teacher, has worked as a personnel officer, and was the Editor of *The New Classic* and *S'ketsh* magazines for some time. He is now the full-time Director of the Federated Union of Black Arts (FUBA). In 1977 he won the Thomas Pringle Award for poetry. He has become one of he most respected South African poets in international literary circles.

Published works

Poetry
Hurry Up To It, Ad. Donker 1975
The Blues is You in Me, Ad. Donker 1976
The Soweto I Love, David Philip & Rex Collings 1977
Children of the Earth, Ad. Donker 1983
ed. Mbulelo Mzamane, *Selected Poems*, Ad. Donker 1984
Novels
The Root is One, Rex Collings 1979, Panafrica Library Nelson 1982
A Ride on the Whirlwind, Ad. Donker 1981

Mongane Serote Born 1944 in Sophiatown, attended school in Alexandra. In 1969 he was detained under the Terrorism Act, and released nine months later, without being charged. After a period of study at Columbia University, he went into exile in Botswana in 1979. There he is active in Pelculef (Pelindaba Cultural Effort) and the Medu Art Ensemble. In 1975 he won the Ingrid Jonker Prize for poetry, and in 1983 the Ad. Donker Prize for his outstanding contribution to Southern African Literature in the decade of the 70s. He is currently in the United Kingdom.

Published works

Poetry
Yakhal Inkomo, кenoster Books 1972, Ad. Donker 1973
Tsetlo, Ad. Donker 1974
No Baby Must Weep, Ad. Donker 1975
Behold Mama, Flowers, Ad. Donker 1978
ed. Mbulelo Mzamane, *Selected Poems*, Ad. Donker 1982
The Night Keeps Winking, Medu Art Ensemble 1982
A Tough Tale, Kliptown Books 1987
Novels
To Every Birth its Blood, Ravan Press 1981
Edited
Shaya: An Anthology of Poetry by South Africans in Exile in Botswana, Pelculef 1977

Mutiswayo Shandu Formerly of Melmoth, KwaZulu, he moved to Pretoria, working as a lawyer's clerk.

Mongane Serote

Can Themba

Published work

'Bye Bye, Overcoat' in *Quarry* 80–82, 1982

Can Themba   (1924–1968) He was born in Marabastad, Pretoria. He won
the first Mendi Memorial Scholarship to study at Fort Hare University
College. He graduated with a first class degree in English, and became a
teacher. After winning a short story competition, he began working for
Drum magazine. One of the 1950s generation of *Drum* reporters and short
story writers, Can Themba was revered and admired by a whole generation
of younger writers. His pieces about Sophiatown, where he lived in what he
called The House of Truth, are legendary. He served in many ways as the
model for character Steven Sithole in Nadine Gordimer's novel *A World of
Strangers* and perhaps also for Gideon Shibalo in her *Occasion for Loving*. In
1963 he exiled himself to Swaziland, where he taught for some time. Before
his death his writings were banned in South Africa, but the publisher David
Philip was successful in having them unbanned in 1982.

Published works

Short Stories and pieces
The Will to Die, Heinemann African Writers Series 1972, David Philip 1982
ed. Essop Patel, *The World of Can Themba*, Ad. Donker 1985

Chris van Wyk   Born 1957 in Newclare, Johannesburg. Matriculated from Riverlea High School. Has worked as a clerk and as a researcher for the South African Council for Higher Education, (SACHED). With Fhazel Johennesse, he was founder and editor of *Wietie* and co-director of Sable Books. He is the present editor of *Staffrider* for Ravan Press. In 1980 he was awarded the English Academy of Southern Africa's Olive Schreiner Prize for his first collection of poems, and in 1982 he won the Maskew Miller Adventure Africa Award for his novel for young adults.

Published works

Poetry
It Is Time to go Home, Ad. Donker 1979
Novels
A Message in the Wind, Maskew Miller 1982

Musaemura Zimunya   Born 1949 in Umtali in Zimbabwe, then Rhodesia. In 1975 he was imprisoned, following a demonstration. Thereafter he went into exile, and studied at the University of Kent in Canterbury. He returned to Zimbabwe as a Research Fellow at the University of Zimbabwe, where he lectures in the Department of English.

Published works

Poetry
Zimbabwe Ruins, Mopani Series, Poetry Society of Zimbabwe 1979
In *Zimbabwean Poetry in English*, ed. Kizito Muchemwa, Mambo Press 1978
in *And Now the Poets Speak* (see below)
Thought-tracks Longmans 1982
Edited
(with Mudereri Kadhani), *And Now the Poets Speak*, Mambo Press 1981
Critical Writing
Those Years of Drought and Hunger, Mambo Press 1982

List of Authors

List of Titles